Instant Cosmic Ordering

Instant Cosmic Ordering

Using your emotions to get
the life you really want – now!

Barbel and Manfred Mohr

HAY HOUSE

Australia • Canada • Hong Kong • India
South Africa • United Kingdom • United States

Published and distributed in the United Kingdom by:
Hay House UK Ltd, 292B Kensal Rd, London W10 5BE. Tel.: (44) 20 8962 1230; Fax: (44) 20 8962 1239. www.hayhouse.co.uk

Published and distributed in the United States of America by:
Hay House, Inc., PO Box 5100, Carlsbad, CA 92018-5100. Tel.: (1) 760 431 7695 or (800) 654 5126; Fax: (1) 760 431 6948 or (800) 650 5115. www.hayhouse.com

Published and distributed in Australia by:
Hay House Australia Ltd, 18/36 Ralph St, Alexandria NSW 2015. Tel.: (61) 2 9669 4299; Fax: (61) 2 9669 4144. www.hayhouse.com.au

Published and distributed in the Republic of South Africa by:
Hay House SA (Pty), Ltd, PO Box 990, Witkoppen 2068. Tel./Fax: (27) 11 467 8904. www.hayhouse.co.za

Published and distributed in India by:
Hay House Publishers India, Muskaan Complex, Plot No.3, B-2, Vasant Kunj, New Delhi – 110 070. Tel.: (91) 11 4176 1620; Fax: (91) 11 4176 1630. www.hayhouse.co.in

Distributed in Canada by:
Raincoast, 9050 Shaughnessy St, Vancouver, BC V6P 6E5. Tel.: (1) 604 323 7100; Fax: (1) 604 323 2600

The authors of this book do not dispense medical advice or prescribe the use of any technique as a form of treatment for physical or medical problems without the advice of a physician, either directly or indirectly. The intent of the authors is only to offer information of a general nature to help you in your quest for emotional and spiritual wellbeing. In the event you use any of the information in this book for yourself, which is your constitutional right, the authors and the publisher assume no responsibility for your actions.

A catalogue record for this book is available from the British Library.

Previously published as *Fühle mit dem Herzen und du wirst deinem Leben begegnen* by KOHA-Verlag GmbH, Burgrain, 2007, ISBN 978-3-867280-25-9.

Translated by: Dennis McAllister, Nick Handforth. www.citylanguages.de

ISBN 978-1-4019-1599-5

Printed and bound in Great Britain by Cromwell Press Group.

'All great discoveries are made by men whose feelings run ahead of their thinking.'
(C. H. Parkhurst)

'Undoubtedly, we become what we envisage.'
(M. Bristol)

'The intuitive mind is a sacred gift and the rational mind is a faithful servant. We have created a society that honours the servant and has forgotten the gift.'
(Albert Einstein)

Contents

Introduction

Part I: Thoughts Produce Feelings

The New Age of Feeling Is Already Upon Us   3

What Turf Has to Do with Our Feelings   6

Thoughts Produce Feelings   9

Those Who Move Hearts Move the World   18

Overwriting Old Feelings   22

The Law of Attraction   32

Thoughts Create Feelings and Feelings Create
Thoughts   37

Our Heart's Desire and the Power of 'No'   42

The Vibration of Our Ego   47

Your Friends Create Along with You   53

Land on Your Feet with Your Feelings   56

What Do I Really Want?   62

The Voice of the Heart   65

Part II: Feelings Produce Thoughts

Feelings in the Unconscious 73
Feelings Want to Be Born 80
Different Types of Feeling 86
Every Feeling Contains Its Opposite 93
The Feeling Heart: Jewish Kabbalah 101
When Experience Has Lost Its Way 105
Freeing Suppressed Feelings 110
You Don't Always Need to Know the Cause 120
Thoughts Are There to Be Created 128
Experiencing – Heaven on Earth 130
You and I – Two Perfect Mirrors 137
Exercises in Feeling for Instant Cosmic Ordering 152
Why Heartfelt Wishes Are Stronger 155
Redefining Working on Yourself: It's Right If It's Fun 162

Part III: Practical Applications

Hotline to the Elemental Power 169
How to Use Negative Feelings 174
The Great Advantage of Crimson Clouds of Feeling 177
Being Allowed to and Having to 180
New Firms in this New Age of Feeling 186
The Last Shall Come First 190
Feeling Your Way to Greater Physical Health 197
Love Is the Strongest Power in the Cosmos 202
Wishing for World Peace 208
How Do You Communicate Love? 214
Appendix: A Reading-Feeling Meditation 219

Introduction

Barbel and Manfred Mohr are married, and that means to each other.

This has to be said explicitly, because you could easily be confused, seeing as the co-author of Barbel's mental power book *Cosmic Ordering for Beginners* is Clemens Maria Mohr, who just coincidentally has the same surname.

While it's known that Barbel's favourite hobby is ordering from the cosmos, for years Manfred has studied the effects of feelings on the fulfilment of desires. Many of his ideas and much of his motivation have developed through seminars run by Waliha Cometti.

Waliha is a spiritual teacher with roots in Sufism, which she mixes with her own perception and personal liberal enhancement (you can find out more at www.waliha.ch). We'd like to thank Waliha here for her incredibly generous permission in allowing us to adapt her approaches. Everyone develops their own approach in any case, according to Waliha Cometti. How can a copyright be put on a universal Oneness which we all draw from in the end? We are thankful for the wisdom and kindness of this perspective.

As Barbel is in no way familiar with Waliha's teachings, but is familiar with many others, this has led to long discussions and to Barbel carrying out experiments on her own personal development and within her relationships. In the end, though, both Manfred and Barbel have sought many different teachings and further methods of self-awareness, and have unearthed some amazing insights into the power of feelings.

Barbel believes that 'using the power of feelings to create your own reality is the tool of the future. We are just at the beginning of our discoveries of all that is possible with feelings and how feelings really function.' Manfred is convinced that 'we find ourselves in the middle of a new Age of Feeling; we just haven't really noticed it yet.'

Our wish for you is that you feel good and enjoy the discovery of the power of your own feelings.

Barbel Mohr
Manfred Mohr

☆ Part I ☆

Thoughts Produce Feelings

The New Age of Feeling Is Already Upon Us

While past decades have been marked by rational understanding and positive thinking, emotional viewpoints have become increasingly important in daily life. Suddenly, the weather report provides us with the 'felt' temperature. We speak less of intelligence quotients (IQ) and more of emotional intelligence quotients (EQ). Whereas we used to say, 'Mull it over,' today we increasingly pose the question, 'How does that feel to you?' All of this evidence seems to point to one thing: at the moment, we find ourselves in a period that is changing its focus from analytical thinking to emotional understanding.

Even the signatures at the bottom of letters have changed. 'Yours sincerely' is out and 'Best wishes' is in. Perhaps the most unusual example can be seen in motorcycle magazines. Where there used to be double-page spreads with close-ups of motorcycles in all their technical detail, today these spreads feature photographs of landscapes with twisting and turning roads, with just a minuscule picture of the motorcycle in the bottom corner. What's on offer is the feeling of freedom instead of objective information about technology and function. So we have a move from intellect to feeling, even in a motorcycle magazine.

We've divided this book into three sections. First we take a look at the intellect and concern ourselves with the fact that thoughts produce feelings. Calm, positive thinking is very important in order for us to resolve our all-too-human and ego-afflicted tendency to judge and view everything negatively. *The ego enjoys the negative, and through this makes itself very important.* Whoever is able, despite all inner resistance, to think more positively than negatively is halfway to happiness. The ego will become more refined and our vibrations will improve.

In the second part of this book we explore how feelings also have a life of their own and aren't consciously dictated by the intellect. We suppress many feelings which are then served back to us by the subconscious, in order to be experienced properly and to come into the light. Again, *the ego not only has a predilection for the negative, but also tends to identify itself with feelings; for this reason, we can't escape negative feelings*. So, in the second part of this book we look more into feelings and try to get closer to this subject emotionally.

Finally, we deal with practical applications in Part III. What effects can feelings have on the body and the physical world? This explores how our health, relationships and the concrete effects of our feelings affect our bodies and our surroundings.

In this book, the focus is on the power of the emotions and how they can help your cosmic ordering. What exactly does it mean to be 'in your heart'? How do the ego and feelings go together? The Talmud says:

Pay heed to your thoughts as they will become words,
pay heed to your words as they will become deeds,
pay heed to your deeds as they will become habits,
pay heed to your habits as they will become your character,
pay heed to your character as this will become your destiny.

Each energy (positive or negative) attracts similar energy (people, actions etc.). And with this, we've already arrived at the well-known law of attraction, which we want to talk about a bit more in a couple of chapters.

> Feelings are becoming ever more present in our lives, and more and more people are on their way to being in harmony with their feelings. Pay attention to your feelings for they form energy and therefore life!

What Turf Has to Do with Our Feelings

If you want to lay turf, you have to rip out the old lawn and put down a good layer of sand and soil before you can lay the new turf; otherwise the old weeds will come up straight away.

It's just the same with feelings. If you just lay new ones on top of the old, the old ones will quickly find their way through again. You have to 'put down a good layer of sand and soil' so the new feelings grow roots quickly and well and the old ones become humus. Then, deep underneath, through life experience, you create the fertilizer for wisdom, thankfulness and a deeper ability to love.

I've tried it, with both turf and feelings. I thought – dim-wittedly – that if I just lay turf on top of the old grass, moss and weeds, then the old plants wouldn't have any more light and would die off. What actually happened, of course, is that the new grass didn't have anything to adhere to, and had to fight its way through the old grass before eventually reaching the soil. And because the soil underneath had always been bad (as it consisted of ground-up construction rubble from the house), the lawn had never been good.

What was completely unexpected to me was that the old grass and weeds simply kept growing underneath. They were completely white, because no sunlight reached them, but they grew on tenaciously.

Then I realized that the same thing goes for feelings. Just covering the old ones up doesn't do any good at all. They grow just as tenaciously beneath. If on the other hand you dig them all out (uproot them) and put down a new, nutrient-rich soil before you cultivate new feelings, then the old junk doesn't come through any more. At most, now and again, a single straggly plant will emerge that can no longer do any harm.

What we hope this book will help you to accomplish is, a) to uproot old feelings and do so easily, b) to prepare your 'soil' for new feelings and c) to plant and cultivate these new, desirable feelings. And, of course, we'll be looking in detail at the contribution feelings make in creating our reality, and how we can use this knowledge to our advantage.

As you can't achieve this when your thoughts are running wildly through your head, an important part of this is communicating with your own heart, because it is there you find buried your feelings and your heart's desires. And we confront our feelings better with our hearts than with our heads.

We have called this book *Instant Cosmic Ordering: Using your emotions to get the life you really want – now!*

for a definite reason. Emotions contribute to our creativity, allowing the whole of life to appear in rich fluorescent colours, whereas purely rational thinking presents life only in black and white.

'Feel good and feel it in your heart' is the motto of this book, and it means: 'Look around right now and give your attention first to your heart and then to something in the room that gives you a good feeling, and enjoy that good feeling for as long as possible.'

With this in mind, feel good while continuing reading.

Just putting a lid on something and suppressing it doesn't help in coming to terms with old feelings. 'Uproot, dig up and sow new seeds from the heart' is the order of the day.

Thoughts Produce Feelings

That feelings are a kind of summarized thoughts, even when sometimes they aren't just thoughts, occurred to Barbel for the first time many years ago:

At the time, I was very young and still extremely inexperienced in regards to esoteric ways of thinking. I was queuing for some event. There was a young lady in front of me, and it was immediately obvious to me that she had an enormous hump on one side. I suspected a bad scoliosis (a close school friend of mine had suffered from the same condition and had always worn a corset in order not to develop a similar hump).

The girl ahead of me had a really extreme hump. I asked myself how it must feel to walk around with such a thing. Then she suddenly started talking to her friend and turned towards her. She stood at a 90-degree angle to me and I could see her face clearly. 'Funny,' I immediately thought. 'Her face doesn't look as if she has a hump. She doesn't look as if she feels the way you'd have to feel if you had such a hump,' I pondered further.

The next thing I immediately asked myself was why I believed that a person's face had to express their fundamental attitude towards life. I studied this girl's eyes and movements more closely, but all I could see was that somehow she beamed an attitude to life free of worry.

'Hmm,' I thought, 'maybe she injured herself doing sports or something, and is wearing a huge bandage there in that spot so that it looks like a hump beneath her winter jacket.' I studied her face once more and found that she didn't look like someone who'd just suffered from pain or an accident. At the same time, I thought I must be going mad, the way I desperately wanted to see the face I expected to see. I pondered away at it and then heaved a deep sigh, because I couldn't solve the puzzle. At that moment, the girl readjusted her scarf, and what I saw was that she had a hood on her jacket. She had obviously just absent-mindedly thrown on her jacket and the hood had landed inside, so that there was a thick bump that looked like a hump. She actually had neither a hump nor a huge bandage, just a clumsily thrown-on winter jacket.

I hardly enjoyed the event, as I was brooding the whole time about how it could be that I had 'read'

that she did not have a hump. As a sceptic, which at
that time I was generally, I really had a lot to learn.

Current science has a few tentative explanations to offer in the meantime. They're called 'mirror neurons'. In a nutshell, researchers have discovered that our subconscious is able to assemble an overall picture based on other people's smallest movements, facial expressions, body language and voice inflection, and then simulate the feelings that the other person has in our own bodies.

If the person you're looking at is sad, but acts happy, then something in you analyses the true feelings of that person and your mirror neurons transmit the same signal, as if you yourself were sad. In other words: *you feel in you how others feel.*

Unfortunately, there was no knowledge of mirror neurons in my childhood, so I was simply puzzled by this encounter. At the time, I reached the conclusion through self-analysis that something in me had somehow 'scanned' this girl and made me able to feel what she felt. And my subconscious apparently knew, based on my few years of life experience at that time, that something didn't quite match up. The girl in the queue back then was certainly the best example for me of my internalizing these things. And while brooding, I came to the conclusion that feelings are a type of collection of thoughts. Many different thoughts and impressions of the most varying kinds are collected together by the subconscious into one 'feeling'. It's the body's way of saving space.

My subconscious recognized the girl's experience and impressions and collected them into a feeling. And this feeling didn't fit the aura of the girl in front of me in the queue. Without having to split the impression into individual thoughts, my feeling reported a general analysis: something doesn't fit together here!

It is, therefore, an art to be able to look at your feelings exactly and organize them. They are the basis of our intuition and our navigation system through life. When we cut ourselves off from our emotions, we always miss our desired goals, because we stop listening to this inner navigation system. Feeling is the voice of the navigation system; when I cut myself off from my emotions, run away from them or suppress them, I cut myself off from my navigation system at the same time.

> In order to get closer to our desired goals in life, we have to explore our feelings exactly, so that we can hear the voice of our navigation system better again.

But feelings aren't absolute or 'more clever than us', because we create them ourselves. They are our collected thoughts. When I wallow in self-pitying thoughts, it has nothing to do with 'I'm getting to know my navigation system better'; it means that I have entered a destination in my navigation system of 'problems, bad mood, faults, illness, separation'. Feelings are our navigation system *and* a compendium of desires at the same time. This makes it all confusing!

> Current feelings, which exist in any given moment, are like the voice of our navigation system that wants to tell us where it wants to go. Our basic outlook on life, in contrast, is the goal towards which our inner navigation system is headed.

Feelings Create Goals

The feelings that are created from moment to moment are the method our sense of wellbeing uses to show us which way to go, what is good for us and what is not. The goal is always one that is indicated by the feelings within us that occur most often. Feelings of separation lead us deeper into loneliness, even when, in our minds, we strongly desire togetherness. Instant cosmic ordering teaches us that when we order something from the cosmos (for instance, togetherness), we can't achieve this when feelings of deficiency and worry overwhelm us. And even if somehow togetherness is delivered in this case, it will come with strings attached.

Paying attention to your feelings requires developing a 'release' process while ordering. You have first to release your worries, doubts and feelings of deficiency. Feelings of truthful anticipation, on the other hand, magnetically pull towards us what we desire in life.

If our feelings of separation are the 'goal' we enter into our navigation system, then our feelings drive us more deeply towards that goal. But how? Take this simple example:

Say we feel lonely and separate from everything. This feeling is our basic attitude to life. Then, say a happy, nice person approaches us and wants to make contact. If our unconscious goal is 'being alone', we will find such a person abhorrent. We'll be scared of them and find their happiness downright suspicious. So we'll scare off this person as quickly as we can. Making contact only works with people who are just as melancholy and in just as bad a mood as we are – but then even that doesn't alleviate the loneliness, as two whingers together will always find ways of annoying each other and break away from each other. Unconscious goal achieved: they're both lonely again.

A person with a basic attitude towards life of security and connectedness, on the other hand, bumps with ease into positive social contact everywhere. So you can see the aspect of 'signpost, navigation system and automatic goal entry in the navigation system' as a rule of attraction too. We'll go into this more later, though.

What many people don't realize is that our 'feeling navigation system' works in two directions. That is to say, decisions based on negative feelings usually navigate us further *away* from that which we want in life, while decisions based on positive feelings bring us closer to that which we wish for.

Naturally, the use of reason is desired here. When we are nearly run over in traffic, the decision to run away is certainly good. I'm talking about less extreme situations. Let's take for example two co-workers who perform the same task within the same company. The first one hates the job, annoys all his co-workers, thinks the boss is unbearable and wants to leave and find a better job. The second co-worker is thankful that she has the job because it gives her a secure base and a livelihood. She makes the best of the job, sees the good sides in all of her co-workers and understands the boss's problems. Suddenly, she hears of a new job possibility that interests and inspires her. She's curious about it and the desire for change develops in her.

Fate will have it that both workers see the same job advert in the newspaper and to go to interview for the new position. Their level of experience is identical. They are both more or less perfect for the new post. If the new boss has a reasonable sense of intuition, whom will he give the job to? The one who wants change out of frustration, or the one who wants change for the joy of a new challenge?

> The universe finds the vibration of happiness more attractive and so offers people with this vibration more opportunities.

The universe works by the same rules as a potential new boss (unless he himself is frustrated and so especially resonates with a frustrated candidate). Generally, though, there's almost no way that someone will offer you a job because he has sympathy with your constant frustration. People will almost always only offer you a job when they see positive potential in you and the desire to give it a go.

In the film *What the Bleep Do We Know!?* (www. whatthebleep.com), scientists report that the conscious mind processes 2,000 bits per second and the subconscious 400 billion bits per second. When compared to the entire system of human perception, taking all processes into account, our *conscious* mind knows almost nothing. And we cannot gain entry to unconscious knowledge through the mind, but only through our feelings. A feeling can contain a package of absolutely infinite amounts of individual impressions and thoughts.

> Our feelings navigate us through life. Follow the feeling of contentedness and you follow the path to yourself and to your highest potential.

Our navigation system also has an automatic 'destination entry'. Repeated thought patterns are collected as a feeling, and it is exactly this feeling that we unconsciously follow to reach our secret destination.

> *'Undoubtedly, we become what we envisage.'*
> *(M. Bristol)*

For example:

• Feel unloved, and you'll be unloved.

- Feel like a victim, and you'll continue to be and become one.
- Feel discriminated against, and you'll be discriminated against by everyone.

This isn't unfair; it's the law of nature. How do you feel when someone with a boot-licking, grovelling posture calls on you and begins every sentence with the words, 'I know that you won't give me what I'm asking for but …'? How much do you really want to give something, no matter what, to this person? No one wants to, and neither does life. You don't have to spell this out, either. The cosmos can sense your basic life-feeling and will give you more of what it thinks you want!

In other words, the more often you moan and feel bad, the more there will be to moan about next week! Life says to you, 'Look, I'll give you everything you want, but I don't understand words or letters. I only know types of thoughts, inner pictures and feelings. Feelings are best, because they put all of your thoughts into a single entity. Or clear thoughts, which simply and clearly stand out for themselves, without being countered by contradictory feelings …'

> Every feeling that you have regularly becomes a permanent subscription to the cosmos! Instant cosmic ordering is most successful when you have the RIGHT emotions connected to your order!

Those Who Move Hearts Move the World

Your mind works to decide what you want to achieve, to formulate clearly what you want (for example, to order from the cosmos). Your mind is not responsible for pulling what you desire into your life. The mind *cannot* create any pull. Only feelings can do that!

For example, a public speaker who speaks only logically and matter-of-factly, creating no feeling whatsoever in his audience, tends to put the audience to sleep. He's quickly forgotten and he does not create a desire for action in his audience. It's the same thing with music: if someone plays technically perfectly, but communicates no feeling through the music, everyone will find it boring. Whoever moves hearts moves the world.

It's the same thing with the cosmos. If I send it my 'order' details without feeling, I spark very little 'universal willingness to act'. Even the cosmos can be bureaucratic and slow.

Let's replace our public speaker with one giving the same speech in a way that communicates waves and mountains of feelings. In the extreme, he'll receive a standing ovation and the people will leave feeling that the emotions he engendered have left an impression on them. Either they'll have to tell someone about the experience immediately, or they'll sing, whistle, dance or think about how they can contribute to what's been said. It's the same with a moving concert where the emotions created express themselves in our gait on the way home, in our conversations after the concert and in our dreams. What touches us moves one or other circles of wisdom. And that which moves people, whether speaker or musician, has a drawing-in effect. The more a person moves hearts, the less he has to advertise. Word-of-mouth always provides him with a full house. The feeling that the speaker sends out creates a pull.

The universe functions in exactly the same way.

> If you want to move the universe, you have to reach it with your feelings.

You have to create word-of-mouth advertising with every heavenly body of energy, so that everything is pulled to you and absolutely wants to contribute to the realization of your goals.

Naturally, you could ask, 'What? Is the universe so petty that it searches out its favourites? I thought that in the all-Oneness everyone was loved just the same.' That's also true. The sun is a good image for this. When it shines, it shines on everyone the same amount. It makes no difference between good and bad, worthy or unworthy. It just shines. And that's always, no matter if it's visible or cloudy or night-time. Only you can decide, however, if you carry the sun in your heart.

In the same way, the power of the universe doesn't stop existing just because you don't notice it. You decide whether or not you carry this elemental power in your heart and use it. Carrying the sun or elemental power in your heart can also be equated with being confident.

Confident people are healthier and live longer. Science has proved this. Without confidence, neither the wheel nor the light bulb nor anything else would have been invented. Without confidence, no one would risk anything and nothing new would come into existence. Confident people make friends and find partners more easily; they find jobs and new places to live more easily. Confidence radiates and infects other people and the universe in the same way. This is the so-called law of attraction. 'Birds of a feather flock together,' goes the saying. Confident people have a positive attracting effect. Confidence is when word gets round the whole cosmos, including every 'universal delivery man', that it's worth delivering to you because you're someone who grabs opportunities and makes the best out of them.

Confidence is a feeling.

And it can be practised.

For everyone.

This is the equal treatment the cosmos gives everyone: The sun shines everywhere, but you have to make use of it.

Pulling the Negative Towards You

All right, all right. Unfortunately, negativity also exists. And is much more strenuous. I like Michael Aivanhov's explanation best, which I've written about in *The Cosmic Ordering Service*: everything that exists is made of light, material things (modern quantum physicists agree with this) as well as situations and feelings and thoughts. Light is the building-block of everything. And the more light a thought or a feeling has, the more building material it contains. Dark thoughts contain little light and so little building material. Therefore, it takes more effort to bring a dark thought into existence than one full of light. But as the feeling causes its own pull, it eventually makes itself noticed.

The soul decides what it wants to accomplish.

Feeling is what creates pull. It causes 'word-of-mouth advertising' in the entire universe and pulls everything in that suits the movement of your feeling.

The sun shines equally on everyone. Everyone decides for themselves whether to stand in the shade or the sunshine. And everyone has the same access to the energy of the elemental power.

Overwriting Old Feelings

Why is the subconscious sometimes so lazy about changing the direction of our life? Because it's so big, that's why. As already mentioned, we process 200 million times more information subconsciously than consciously.

Imagine a small boat in the Antarctic. The captain sees an iceberg appear before him. What does he do? He sails around it – small manoeuvre, no problem. Now let's imagine an enormous tanker. Suddenly, an iceberg appears. The captain signals the alarm and takes the wheel. The information is sent to the rudder. Sluggishly and slowly, the huge rudder sets itself into motion, and by the time the entire tanker has changed its course, the ship's run into the iceberg.

A small ship is flexible and can change course in seconds; a giant supertanker is inflexible and extremely slow in correcting its course.

The human system processing its 400 billion bits of information per second is similar to a sluggish tanker. Except – and this is the crucial difference – the human system is capable of fusing for a moment into a single unit when strong emotions are involved. When this happens and the person is receptive from their big toe through their heart and soul to the ends of their hair, then veering around the iceberg in seconds is suddenly possible.

Feelings can make a manoeuvrable motorboat out of any sluggish tanker. The right feeling can also 'reformat' and 'overwrite' entire parts of the human hard drive lickety-split.

I remember a married couple who came to me for advice. The wife was given to extreme fits of rage. She could scream and rant and smash half the furniture. It looked like an unresolvable fixed programme of hers, until the day her husband discovered how to reformat it. She was ranting in the kitchen one day, smashing plates, when he came in very quietly and said, 'I promised at our wedding to love you the way you are. I guess I have to love this too.' She paused a moment and stared at him amazed and totally flabbergasted. It sank in. And that was the end of all her extreme rages. Just one remark and she was done with it. Of course, she could still be a bit angry, but much more measured and she never destroyed anything in a rage again.

We can see from this how important feelings are. Feelings connect and can create wholeness. Connectedness, wholeness, security, togetherness don't allow themselves to be debated, they are based on feelings. Exactly these qualities are what we need to acquire peace and a readiness to co-operate in groups and teams at work and in our private lives. And we need them just as much for peace and a readiness to co-operate to exist between our cells and our conscious or between our subconscious and our conscious. Without reaching our feelings, we can't make any progress.

How do we reach our feelings? There are many possibilities and it doesn't matter how we begin: every beginning and every aim will expand and grow. We can then begin to change our inner communication, and, by means of repeated thought patterns, overwrite our feeling patterns piece by piece. Instead of thinking, 'I hate that old pot; it's always burning things,' you can change your inner communication to, 'I love that old pot; it's original.' You won't notice anything at first and will think it's not helping, but when you really have the intention to be more loving, then things begin to change. Suddenly, someone will give you an amazing new pot, and you'll realize that, without noticing, the old pot has grown on you. You don't want to toss it out any more, and instead use it as a pot for a beautiful flower on the windowsill.

Or say you've repeatedly tended to notice the bad qualities in your partner. 'Why does he always wrinkle his nose so stupidly whenever he wants something from me? What a dimwit.' New aim, new formulation: 'I love the way he always wrinkles his nose so adorably.' You won't notice anything at first, but bit by bit you'll overwrite that feeling of annoyance. Then all of a sudden, you'll notice that you hardly even notice him wrinkling his nose any more. Somehow, it's disappeared from your consciousness. Instead, a comforting shiver will run through you when you think about how wonderfully co-operative your partner is. And perhaps you'll have also forgotten that only a few months ago he wasn't really that way. The feeling of oneness is just stronger in your relationship. And it all began with just a small aim that you didn't have much faith in the changing power of, because you sensed absolutely nothing. But the change sneaked in anyway.

The more you practise such things, the more you develop your power and feeling, and the more feelings will come to you that you can use at the right moment to permanently change a negative situation into a positive one.

Negative feelings disturb the metabolism, weaken the immune system and make us lethargic and react more sensitively to stress, because negative thoughts and feelings themselves produce stress hormones. Every external stress is then just extra stress.

Positive feelings can erase and reverse the effects of negative feelings within seconds. It's like a student at school who hates maths and finds himself at the beginning of a double maths lesson. Somehow, almost all his spirit flags and he feels tired, demotivated and frustrated, and thinks, 'I won't understand anything again anyway …' Even the immune system and metabolism flag when a person feels this way.

Suddenly, there's an announcement over the PA system: 'Classes suspended due to the cold. Every student can go home now.' It takes only a fraction of a second for our previously totally lethargic maths student to be wide awake and excited. Why? Because he has a positive feeling again. At that moment, the metabolism, immune system etc. are at full power again.

If only for the sake of our physical health, we should pay attention to cultivating positive feelings. Because in most everyday situations, we have a *choice* in how we want to feel. The increased positive feelings make us healthier, allowing our intuition to function better and everything to go more smoothly.

(If you want to read more about this process, we'd recommend Thomas Klüh's book *Erfolgsgefühle – Die emotionalen Grundlagen des Erfolges* [*Feelings of Success*], Werner Ablass's *Leide nicht – liebe* [*Love, don't suffer*] and Esther and Jerry Hicks's *Ask and It Is Given*.)

Begin with overwriting habitual bad feelings with more positive ones.

Take responsibility for your experience every day and at every moment. Concentrate on developing a loving attitude.

Even if you don't notice some changes immediately, they will break though sooner than you might expect.

Every time you allow a positive feeling from head to toe, you hold the power in your hands to rewrite your life!

Overwriting Deep-rooted Moods

An especially beneficial feeling to have is that of playful, childlike lightness, naturalness and joy in being. The basis on which to achieve this are the feelings of *love*, *freedom* and *appreciation*. Children are born with these feelings. I haven't yet seen a baby who offers its mother a cold grimace when she smiles lovingly. Babies automatically bring appreciation, joy and love with them into the world. Babies also have a feeling of freedom in them: the freedom to express themselves the way they are at any moment. No baby thinks when it's hungry whether it's the right time to get mother to feed it. The baby expresses its needs freely and without reservation. This is the type of inner freedom that I mean.

It's best to start from the bottom up. Say someone is down in the depths of the worst depression and can't even imagine that there are people out there who really feel free and happy. Depressed and melancholy people very honestly presume that every type of joy is basically fake, and that somewhere beneath must lie a real world-weariness. In such a case, you can first define for them what the 'most realistic, still possible positive attitude to life' is – one that even they can just about believe in, so that it is achievable. Writing it down can be helpful. And when they've achieved that, they can allow themselves perhaps to create new goals.

How Do I Achieve My Ideal Feeling for Life?

EXERCISE 1

It can be easier than you think right now. Make a list of all the possible feelings you can think of from the bottom up: from anger, annoyance, hate, trust to boredom, satisfaction and calm to euphoria, sympathy, love, joy and whatever else occurs to you.

Then think about which feelings are achievable for you at the moment, the ones that feel better to you than the ones you have now. We know from traditional therapy that depressives, as they slowly emerge from their lethargy, often become angry and aggressive. If you should meet someone like that, try to understand that they don't mean it in a bad way, and try to not take it badly. Because, relative to depression, anger and aggressiveness are an improvement! A person who's angry feels better than a person stuck in a depression. My tip on this: Don't feel personally affronted by this behaviour, instead see the anger as a self-protection mechanism against depression.

If you're the one who wants to get out of depression, and you feel the first refreshing life-signs of anger or impatience in yourself, here's my tip: don't shout at whomever's frustrating you. Instead, take a big cushion, stick a picture or the name of the person to it and let off steam on the cushion. This isn't a joke. When an hour later you meet your boss whom you've just 'worked over' in private, you'll be able to smile with a feeling of 'I've already served you up yours today. Now I can be gracious and smile ...'

EXERCISE 2

Another example: You're scared of someone or a certain situation, and are sick to your stomach every time you have to confront it. There's no set rule, but we can look a bit at NLP (neuro-linguistic programming) for help here. NLP helps us to shrink all the disturbing thoughts and mentally strengthen the thoughts we desire. If you can also *feel* them, it is a very powerful exercise.

Try to imagine a fantasy picture of the person or situation that scares you – but in this case, the fear dissolves:

- Your scary boss is a ladybird sitting on the desk and you are normal-sized in front of her.
- Imagine the almighty person with diarrhoea. Every time they want to be unfriendly, it hits them and they have to run to the toilet. Sometimes we forget that we're just people with totally normal, human needs. A small reminder of how we're basically all human and the same in this way can be very calming (and empowering!).
- When you feel like an outsider, imagine that a small army of 20 more 'outsiders' are with you. Accompanied by your co-outsider friends, the other person is always outnumbered.
- Exam fear: imagine there's a secret 'bonus exam' running parallel to the main exam. Whoever is the most relaxed during the bonus exam, no matter how poorly he does, scores the most points. Or imagine yourself coming back from ten years in the future and doing

the exam calmly, because the future you has more life experience, knowledge and composure.

- A woman wanted to get rid of all her anger towards her ex-husband. Every time he picked up the kids, her blood boiled. By getting her to picture her ex as an animal (she chose a rat!), I helped her get to the point where she was no longer so angry with him. Every time he stood in front of her she just imagined he was a sewer rat, and the image was so funny she had to relax. Of course, you can also play this game for the positive. In this instance I asked the woman to imagine the ideal relationship, and after she described it to me, I asked her if she could imagine an animal that lived that way. A dolphin was the answer. So, I said, she should imagine herself as a dolphin every morning, and every evening she should imagine herself pleasurably swimming around with her dolphin partner.

These are all picture aids with which we produce entirely new feelings in a childlike way.

And there's only one rule in this game: fantasize as long as you need to until you find a picture that feels good to you. Write it down and visualize it every morning and every night before you fall asleep. Your feelings will change to positive ones, and you'll be stronger and feel lighter at the same time.

If your problem is just that you're not really happy and you feel a bit numb – no anger, no depression, nothing bad, but still no real happiness – then just keep a conscious lookout for feelings that are better and more alive than the ones you have at present.

- When you see a laughing child, try to put yourself in the place of the child and feel the joy with her.
- When you see a madly dashing dog, put yourself in his place and feel the joy of the power and the movement.
- Get out into the countryside to feel the connection to the power of Creation.
- Keep a lookout for the smallest things which you can be thankful for and which you can be happy about.

What is the 'most real' imaginable positive feeling to you at this moment? Aim for that, and keep a lookout for the next positive imaginable feeling at the moment. Move ahead step by step.

When a situation or a person presents you with difficult problems, create a fantasy picture with which you can change the situation or person so that they become harmless.

Example: dangerous bosses or hated ex-partners become harmless when you shrink them down to insect-size.

The Law of Attraction

Have you experienced this? Something bad happens to you in life and suddenly you're scared of experiencing it again. When I was a child, for example, a dog bit me once while I was out walking. Now, every time I'm walking alone in the park and a loose dog comes running up to me, I get scared. Silly, really, as I'm twice as tall now as I was when I got bitten – but tell that to my fear!

Fear – and really all negative feelings like anger, rejection, inadequacy, depression etc. – are not independent of us, but a part of us. And that part is our *ego*. Our ego has nothing better to do than search out the negative in order to make it important. And the ego always finds something. That much is certain. Because the ego only wants one thing: to inflate itself and us. Because no one is as pitiful as me. And, on the other side, no one's *sooo* great as me either.

It is precisely for this reason that so many people feel that only negative news is 'real' news. If the ego of the entire human population improved itself, among other things it would recognize that more positive news is needed. *But the bigger the ego, the more uninteresting it finds positive news and the more it loves generating fear.* Fear is just one of those things. It has its own special energy, and this energy is not really very constructive. In any case, it attracts further, equally bad, energy. We notice this when we walk across a park and a dog runs up to us. It can smell from a distance if we're scared. And if we're scared, it'll growl. And if we're *really* scared, it'll bark. Or even bite. But we knew that!!! Dogs bite. The silly thing is that if we weren't scared, the dog wouldn't have growled and would definitely not have bitten. That's true, isn't it? So, what was the decisive factor in what happened? Our energy! And this is shaped by our feelings.

Of course, you're now saying, fine; but the universe isn't a dog! In a certain sense, though – and we're sorry about this – it is! Because it assumes we know the law of attraction, and become scared because we want to experience being bitten by a dog. The universe doesn't judge. It looks at us, really studies us, and like the dog, recognizes 'Aha, this person is afraid, fear equals a lot of energy, so what's all this actually about? Aha, a lot of energy is being focused on getting bitten. Fine, here you are!'

In order to move away from negative feelings to something a bit more pleasant, we'll take the feeling of determination as our next example: 'I know what I want.' Imagine yourself in a situation where you know exactly what you want! Feel yourself into it and imagine it in all its detail. Really take your time. (Take a short break. You can go to the fridge or the bathroom and still do the exercise at the same time.) Wow! Great energy!

Do you know who is really good at showing us if we are in a state of good, focused energy? Horses! A few years ago, I (Manfred) took part in a horse seminar. There was absolutely no riding involved, all you had to do was to walk around the paddock to see if the horse followed you. If you were full of focused energy, the horse would follow you, as if pulled by a magnet. But if a person was even a little uncertain, the horse would just sniff the person a bit and then act as if the person didn't interest it in the slightest. Dieter, Barbel's co-trainer from her vitality seminars (he has been a professional trainer for decades and holds a two-hour guest seminar in Barbel's programme), came to participate for a short time during this horse seminar. Dieter, it seems, was born with determination. In reality, he was once the exact opposite. It took him many years to develop this powerful state. When Dieter went into the paddock, the horse stood stock still, caught his scent and then stuck to Dieter's heels. It wouldn't leave his side. Dieter laughed and insisted that he hadn't done a thing.

It not something that you can do, it is something you have to be. It's really fascinating to experience. A horse can actually smell our power, just like a dog senses our fear.

There are also many analogies, which can be applied to people. In interviews, future bosses decide on who will get the job within the first few minutes. Within this short period, the candidate has hardly had time to open their mouth to say 'Hello,' and has probably only listened to the description of the position. During blind dates, often the first seconds, the 'first look', decide if there's to be a relationship or not. Successful businesspeople decide on important things through gut feeling and not with their heads. People who buy shares on the stock market through feeling are often more successful than those who scrutinize all the stock-market figures.

Why is this? Because there's more to us than normal human comprehension will allow us to believe. We know from wave theory that waves can strengthen energy. This is why it is necessary for an army to march across a bridge out of step; otherwise the bridge will begin to sway, which could be dangerous. The effect depends on the bridge's own movements, and when these movements 'hit a resonance' with the movement of the marching group, it can build up dangerously. Similarly, the 'resonance principle' means that when like energies meet in resonance, they can build up and strengthen. So, for example, if my fear of the biting dog is big enough, then my ego will look for the corresponding energy: neither a nice poodle nor a gentle St Bernard will run up to me in the park, but a rather dangerous pit bull.

If I live in a terraced house and fear burglars, which house is the burglar going to seek out?

If I have a child and fear that it will stumble, what will happen?

If I fear a shortage of money, what will happen?

If I fear losing a partner ...

If I fear losing my job ...
If I fear illness ...

Your basic life attitude decides whether the dog that approaches you snarls or wags its tail.

Your fundamental life attitude decides whether people follow or turn away from you.

And so it will go with the whole of life: jobs, partners, money and situations.

Thoughts Create Feelings and Feelings Create Thoughts

Imagine that you're a factory. Just like a factory, you take in things (food, water, air) and, with the aid of diverse materials, produce your own products (energy, metabolism, hormones, heartbeats, lung movement …). Waste is also created: sweat and other excretions. This is just the visible arena, though. Besides this, you also sense your environment (eyes, ears, all the senses), certain feelings in other people, voices; and process them. And, of course, you are also sending out your own thoughts and feelings into your environment.

Now, you're not alone in this great big world. There are a few million others scattered across this globe, and where feelings and thoughts are concerned, we all do the same thing: we take in feelings and then release some. Seen in terms of energy, we 'resonate' at certain frequencies, we take in resonance and give off resonance too. And, naturally, we are influenced by the resonance of others, just as we influence others through our resonance. At the same time, people in our immediate surroundings are more strongly influenced by us, and, naturally, the people closest to us take in more of our resonance.

To recognize this shows us our freedom, but at the same time our responsibility too: nothing can happen to us which doesn't exist in our field of resonance. It has to have something to do with us, even if we don't understand it at first glance. And we have every freedom to choose our frequency and, through free will, to change it again and again. We can choose our surroundings, we can become clear through our thoughts, and we can look more closely at our feelings.

With that we take a decisive step closer to who we really are: free and creative! When we're successful in freeing ourselves from more and more of the shackles of our old thought processes, then we recognize that we ourselves are responsible for that which surrounds us and happens to us. And that we have the freedom to change all of this with instant cosmic ordering, the steering wheel of our thoughts and the engine of our feelings.

Thoughts create feelings and feelings create thoughts. It is just as important to be clear about your goal and to organize your thoughts as it is to care for the engine and to aim at the important emotional power in order to fulfil your wishes. Learning the power of positive thinking is more or less the basis or foundation to turning them towards more positive feelings.

Some people who might, full of enthusiasm, be marvelling at the moment at the enormous power of feelings probably believe that humanity has made a mistake in the past in engaging our mental powers only. They forget, though, that thoughts create feelings, or at least an important part of them. Thoughts that are repeated over and over become feelings in the end. Feelings are a type of compressed memory of thoughts. Feeling, additionally, shows us how connected we are with the elemental power, and navigates us towards our heart's desires.

So it isn't a choice between feelings or thoughts: both belong together.

The term 'feeling' needs to be looked at a bit closer here. In normal usage, 'feeling' is, confusingly, used to express the similar concepts of sensation, impression and emotion. The psychologist Carl Jung, for example, found four basic human functions, which he defined in this way:

1. **Sensation/experience** establishes what actually exists.
2. **Thinking** enables us to recognize the *meaning* of what exists.
3. **Feelings** show us what the thing which exists is *worth* to us.
4. **Intuition** allows us to sense which *possibilities* are currently available to us. (Source: C.G. Jung, *Collected Works*, Volume 6).

In that first moment when an initial impression of something is communicated through our feelings (Jung would call this *sensation* or *experience*), this feeling is intuitive and genuine: How does it make me feel? There is no active thought, just an openness to input. It's almost animal, primal. It may even be that animals are always in the 'How does it feel?' mode. 'How does it feel?' brings us closer to our source, our beginning, and what we are there has a lot to do with our Self, with that which we really are. It is the condition of the Garden of Eden before the apple of knowledge (that is to say, our minds) entered the stage: I feel this way! And it's different for each person. Everyone experiences and feels things differently, and even the same person can feel differently tomorrow from how he does today. Thoughts and assessment only come later.

When we're connected to our feelings (with pure emotion), we are always in the now. And that's certainly the best place we can be. There's no room for grief from yesterday or worries about tomorrow. This is what it is now! And in three seconds, a new now! And then different again and yet again. To be in our feelings is to be in the river of life, to put the plug in the mains socket, to be connected to the power. How is it? Aha, like that! It's being connected to the source that shows us 'This feels good, I want that' and 'That felt bad, I'd rather not have it.' In this 'heart-feeling', being is always primal, as such a feeling is always right, it flows from the well of our immortal being. Now I feel like this! This feeling can be uncomfortable, but it can never be false. It always provides us with meaningful feedback. It doesn't make mistakes.

Our feelings are the entrance to our true selves, our wishes and our purpose. When we train these very weakened feeling muscles and listen more and more to them, a new, infinite world opens up! Through our sensations we are connected with everything, with every person, with animals, plants, with nature; we can even learn how to feel mountains and water. Behind this are sensitivity and fine perception, which increasingly allow us to appreciate what is really around us.

> When we pay more attention to our feelings, for example by looking at our inner life more often, we get to know ourselves better and become more authentic. We get closer to our real selves again and sense ourselves again, instead of making a mental exercise out of who we should, could or are allowed to be.
>
> Being in feeling mode is always primal, because our sensations are always right; they flow from the well of our immortal being.

Our Heart's Desire and the Power of 'No'

What Do You Really, Really Want?

Our heart's desire has its source in our deepest soul. It is the answer when we ask ourselves honestly, 'What do I really want?' And for this it needs a clear feeling. Then a wish has power. If you've learned to go deep and really feel what's inside, then you find something in you that is completely attached to you. Your heart will then give you an answer.

A wish from the heart is stronger than a wish purely from the mind, which can be very superficial. A wish from the heart exists in a mood of unending love and gratitude for the universe. The feeling of love and gratitude has the highest movement or frequency (Masaru Emoto in his book *Messages from Water* was able to demonstrate this impressively with his water crystals). A wish sent to the cosmos needs to be done when you are totally in the now, in the feeling, and therefore committed to your source of being. Even if it is just for a short moment, you've wished and ordered in that tenth of a second with the complete naïveté and impartiality

of a newborn, without doubt, just immersed in the feeling of 'How beautiful; I want that now.' For a short moment, the entire creative force of the universe unfolds, because you are connected to the creative source, to love and gratitude.

Through this feeling you can connect to the 'creative broadcaster', moving endless power and energy in a single moment. Everything is possible in this short moment. This single moment is enough.

When Instant Ordering Doesn't Seem to Work

When an order doesn't go very well, often it's because it wasn't a real wish from the heart. And often the reason for this is that you weren't completely immersed in a feeling of love and gratitude, but in a feeling of inadequacy instead. You could also say, 'I ordered something unconsciously that I really *didn't* want.' Sounds silly? Let's take a look.

Let's go back to the biting dog again: I'm scared that the dog will bite me. So I'm in the 'That dog's about to bite me' mode. This frequency attracts all the biting dogs in the park. The reason for this is actually my own unconscious wish which could be summed up as: 'Oh no, how awful, a park. I hope another loose pit bull doesn't come running up to me.'

Most of us have heard that we should avoid negatives and the words 'no' and 'not' when we are instant cosmic ordering, because the unconscious doesn't hear the negative. It accepts the 'bigger picture' of the thought as the request.

But if we go a step further and look at what the phrase 'I hope a dog doesn't bite me again' sends out emotionally, we see that it *is* a clear feeling: no way and no how do I want to be bitten! This is a clear feeling of 'I *don't* want that,' but feeling-wise I'm still in 'be bitten' mode, because I can very strongly feel how it was back then when the dog bit me and hurt me.

> It is very important to look honestly at what feeling you are really in at the moment you wish for something and place your cosmic order.

It's the same thing when you order from a place where you feel inadequate. Perhaps I'm in debt and desperately need money. Perhaps I'm unemployed and looking for a job. Perhaps I'm alone and looking for a partner. Perhaps I'm ill and want to be healthy. In all of these examples, we run the risk of creating a feeling of inadequacy, and that has no power. For this reason, it's good to accept things as they are now first, and then to order.

So, just as a deeply sad composer can't compose an 'Ode to Joy', a melancholy painter can't paint a picture that expresses light, and a poet who's angry can't write a romantic love poem. The same goes for you: when you're in a bad mood, you can't create positive life changes!

No matter whether you're working on a piece of music, a painting, a poem, or your daily life: *your feeling finds its place in all you do!*

Let's take the example of bringing up children. Suppose a mother says to her young child: '*Don't* knock over that cup!' The child's unconscious doesn't hear the *don't*. The instruction causes the child immediately to have a picture of a knocked-over glass in his head. He can't help it.

In childrearing, we underestimate how this need to think about what we hear and how the *don't* in the sentence strengthen the thought! So when Mum says, '*Don't* knock over that cup!' feelings take this as an order to, in fact, knock over the cup, because feelings react to the inner image that this command evokes. The child sees the knocked-over cup in his head and uses this command to do exactly that. The child and his feelings naturally want to do right by Mum, and make a great effort to throw the cup. As soon as he does this, the child is reprimanded or even punished. It may be that the child's mind understands this and finds it logical somehow. Feelings do not, however. Mum has created a picture through her command and the child has done what his unconscious feels his mum's asked him to do, then he's punished.

Feelings don't understand this. There's a twist in the feeling, because feelings and the mind want completely different things.

The solution would be for the mum to rephrase her admonishment: 'Leave the cup where it is. Be sure that it stays upright!' Using this formulation, the meaning remains the same for both feelings and the mind and there isn't any confusion.

You can easily see with this example that more is achieved with feeling than with the mind. *Feelings react to inner images.* They are resolved through words, among other things, but follow subtler laws than the mind does.

Formulating goals that contain negatives can lead to confusing your feelings. Feelings react to inner images. Saying, 'Don't knock over the cup,' leads to a clear image of a knocked-over cup. Then when we encounter anger because the cup has been knocked over, our feelings become confused and stifle our inner creativity, because that part of us doesn't understand what went wrong.

The Vibration of Our Ego

What do we really want in life? To be happy and lead a nice life, and preferably to share it with all of the people around us! When we know more about the universal laws of attraction and reaction, then it's clear that, like a magnet, our aura and base energy pull people and events into our lives that correspond to us or our energy. Realizing this is the equivalent of taking complete and total responsibility for ourselves. It also means giving up the role of victim and no longer putting the blame on anyone else for the state of your life: not your parents, not your partner, not the children nor anyone else. It means, instead, recognizing more and more the creative power within us and learning to use this energy to get ourselves on the right path. And it means, above all else, the willingness to work on ourselves.

The more we vibrate, the more energy we have, the more nice and pleasant things and events we pull into our lives. The more we vibrate, the more often we are 'in our heart' and so able to send out our heart's desires, which then have the power to become reality. So, back to work!

If we do something good for ourselves, we often think – and, above all, feel – positively. This increases our energy even more! Sure, sometimes it's not so easy in practical life. Because we have something within us that really likes to speak to us in order to get attention, and that's our ego. Working on ourselves means refining our ego. I'd compare it internally with a predator that would like to be reined in by its tamer.

You can recognize very practically in everyday behaviour just how sophisticated the ego is. It displays itself especially in criticizing and pointing out faults and weaknesses in others. Besides this, it wants recognition of and agreement with others in its opinion. The ego displays its tendency to want to bring others to its own opinion, and wants to force its offer of help or knowledge on others. The ego also wants to be right in the case of disagreements. The ego wants to assert itself.

You can recognize most clearly how refined or unrefined your ego is by the way in which you deal with mistakes. The ego strives for perfection; it wants to be first and best. The open heart is welcoming and loving, the opposite of censorious and critical. The ego defines itself by making others feel bad. If you can stand being small sometimes, then it's an important step in taming your ego.

Whoever can stand by their mistakes, and accept and respect the mistakes of others, is really on the path to refining their ego.

The ego, of course, will put up enormous resistance to your attempts at making it finer and more transparent. In order to open your heart, it is important always to recognize this resistance, and then tell your ego, 'The reality is there, it's happened. It makes no sense to fight against it. It's just the way it is. I don't understand it, but I accept it.' In other words, to learn to say, 'That which is, is good.' And even when you don't care for it, it has to be right and good somewhere, because it obviously exists. Fighting against it would be pointless. (Byron Katie, the founder of *The Work* says, 'When I argue with reality, I lose – but only 100 per cent of the time.')

This is not as hard as it sounds. Accepting the world as it is doesn't mean that we have to let it stay that way. Working on something new is wonderful. Wanting to battle against what is drains you of your energy and changes absolutely nothing. The mantra 'It is what it is' is a trick to escape the limited viewpoint of the ego and to achieve an 'entireness' which is like a blank slate to be written on again. When the opinion of the ego is put at rest, the path is free to the truth and knowledge of the heart.

In the best-case scenario, this helps you make sense of the past. There's no more opinion on that which has happened; it was how it was and there's no placing blame any more. The now is accepted (it is what it is), and with it the path to every future we may want to achieve is cleared. There are no more thoughts stuck in the past; when we speak of the past, it is only to share certain things with others as an example or to help them learn. As long as we go back to thoughts of the past with feelings of judgement and guilt, our energy stays in the past and can develop no power in the future or in the now. Such a person hasn't conquered their present because they haven't conquered their past.

Are You Still Living in the Past?

How can you recognize if you are still living in the past? This reveals itself if you always talk about the past, think about the past and daydream about how things used to be. Some people constantly complain and rant about the old days, parents, exes, former bosses or family members. They constantly bring up what's happened in the past, don't talk about anything else and begin to develop a certain pleasure in this unhappiness, this sense of not being fulfilled, because the ego then gets to say, 'No one is worse off than me.' In this way the ego can inflate itself.

Speaking negatively forces other people into this energy, as everyone has an ego. You have to first learn to protect yourself from such energies. Negativity is a kind of emergency backup generator, when there are too few positive vibrations available to be connected to the heart and the cosmos where we should, in fact, be getting our power.

We also know from psychoanalysis that everything we value and devalue outwardly is in most cases just a projection of our own insufficiencies and mistakes. Somehow, there's only a make-believe border between the 'I' and the 'you'. We are all connected. Making others feel bad doesn't do us any good at all. And yet we cheerfully continue to project our insecurity on others.

We also reflect our heart's desire on others. Positive properties are reflected when we are newly in love; after this initial falling-in-love period is over, we do just the opposite by reflecting our darker side onto our partner. We also proceed in the exact same way with our neighbours, co-workers, bosses, friends and colleagues. We make others feel bad to try to make ourselves feel better.

Another favourite and not to be overlooked projection field for what's bad is – the weather! First it's too wet, then too cold, then too windy, then too dry and too hot. We see negative things in the government, our tax returns, our football club, in politics and the whole world. The ego loves negative things, not least on television and in newspapers – that's why the news is full of them. The ego enjoys complaining and groaning. It becomes a certain dependence, even a kind of addiction, especially when a person has grown up and lived with this energy for decades. People are programmed to find what is well known, familiar and safe and, as a rule, become scared about doing something new or leaving their emotional comfort zone. There is an adherence to the emotionally known, and this also works then at the physical level, on the hormones and the metabolism.

We can also derive a kind of vibration pattern from what we already know – that is, from our bio-rhythms. Life doesn't behave uniformly, like the straight lines of geometry, but always in waves. When it comes to the growth and refining of the ego, we create high crests, then fall into troughs again. But, as a consolation, all natural processes run exponentially, like algae growth in a lake, at first indiscernible and slow, then terrifically quick.

To end the chapter, the major question: how do we know when the ego is getting smaller and smaller? When we enter more and more into our heart. Then we find joy in the love and praise of beauty; then we suddenly open our eyes and maybe recognize for the first time the beauty around us: flowers, nature, people, things. Then we enter more and more into being grateful for our existence and the possibilities which life offers us.

The ego likes to moan. It likes to bad-mouth others in order to feel better about itself.

At the same time, though, it can't deal with criticism.

Practise catching your ego out: observe yourself. Admit when your ego has full control of you. Smile internally at such moments and imagine: 'There you are, dear ego, again. How wonderfully you are moaning again. I understand that it makes you fee important ...'

Say to yourself at the same time: 'Never mind, dear ego. I love you nevertheless, and I love myself nevertheless. And now I will see what I feel I would really like to do next, now that I have caught us both red-handed.'

This affectionate introspection will refine the ego fast and efficiently.

Your Friends Create Along with You

Noel Edmonds, the well-known English TV presenter, writes in his book *Positively Happy* that there are people who spread the lore of how bad they're doing so widely that they eventually acquire a secret title. When friends and acquaintances speak about this person, they no longer speak about 'Bob' any more, for example, but about 'Poor Bob'.

They speak in low voices when they talk about this 'Poor Bob' who's always doing badly. If they meet Bob somewhere, they most likely don't address him directly as 'Poor Bob,' but they don't trust themselves to ask outright, 'Hey, mate, why are you always like this?' Instead, in a subdued tone and with a sympathetically wrinkled forehead, they ask in a concerned voice, 'So, Bob, how are you?' The problems with doing this are:

- **Your basic life-feeling creates your reality;** many people know this, and
- **your subconscious listens to and strengthens what you say about your life.**

- In 'Poor Bob's' case from Noel Edmonds's book, Bob has caused a part of his environment **to strengthen this effect. It now sends an additional message to the universe: 'That's Bob who's always doing poorly.'**

So Bob's well-meaning friends, in fact, actively support him in creating a one-way road into a cul-de-sac that connects 'misery' and 'Bob' together.

If you think you might have earned this kind of secret title, then you should retrain your friends and acquaintances as quickly as possible. New training goal: 'Bob is the one who always enjoys life, no matter what's happening' and 'Bob is the one who stands tall after every crisis.' If there's to be a title, then rather 'Bob, our new phoenix' than 'Bob, our Eeyore' or something to that effect.

EXERCISE

In order to get to know yourself a bit better, and to see where you're going internally, you can do a little test:

1. What's your favourite animal? Write it down, and write down everything that you especially like about the animal. Why is it your favourite animal?
2. What's your second favourite animal? Write this down too, and write down what you like about it.
3. Finally, what's your third favourite animal? What do you like best about it?

Solutions

Animal 1: Your self-image.

Animal 2: The image that others have of you – and that you may want to correct – and that will help you to see the kind of feelings you are projecting out into the world.

Animal 3: Your ideal picture of yourself. The way you wish to be.

If it's become habit for you to allow others to pity you, you have, in fact, in energy terms engaged them in continuing to keep you that way.

Examine your self-perception and how you really want to be. Display your best characteristics to the world and forbid your ego from moaning and complaining. Direct your attention instead to the things that go well and share these positive moments, no matter how small they may be, with your friends.

Land on Your Feet with Your Feelings

We find it totally normal in our society to keep negative feelings internalized, to mull them over and give them a lot of attention. Positive situations, however, we quickly dismiss as 'kitsch' or 'naff', and even avoid them or do our best to get away from them.

For instant cosmic ordering purposes, this is exactly the wrong way round. If we want to achieve positive things, we should dwell *especially* on positive feelings and leave the negative ones as quickly as possible by the wayside.

In order to get to a better feeling through the power of thought, which then attracts more comfortable conditions, there are a few interesting tricks you can use. Albert Einstein said that you cannot solve problems at the same level at which they were created. This is why it is so important to increase our vibrations in order to approach problems with better energy. Above all, it is important to recognize that dwelling on your problems helps not at all, or at least very little, in solving them innovatively.

The problem will only be energetically strengthened and then the negative aspect of the problem will keep running through your head.

Einstein also lets us know that all nature tends towards harmony. That means that you don't *have* to solve *every* problem, and that sometimes it's enough to just stop thinking about it constantly. We can then give nature room within us to move towards harmony.

The nature of the entire cosmos is creative, and we can trust in it – but it can only help us when we leave the energy of our problems behind. We then open the doors to the cosmos:

- You can think about something nice instead (holiday, partner, hobby, children …)
- You can talk yourself out of a problem as you would speak to a child. ('It'll be all right,' 'Everything will be fine,' 'Everything will look different tomorrow …')
- You can rationally say to yourself, 'I know from experience that if I stay in this energy, it'll bring me nothing, because I'll just keep pulling the same nonsense into my life …'
- You can do something nice for yourself (see a film, meet friends, go for a walk …)
- You can look at what makes you happy, and follow your happiness.

And, in emergencies, you can make a 'feel-good' list, which you carry around with you everywhere (in your wallet, for example). A feel-good list should include all of the things that cause warm, happy feelings when you think about them. This could be:

- people
- things
- events
- beautiful pieces of clothing or a football match won
- special situations
- places in nature.

When you find yourself in a low mood, get your list out and direct your attention to something on it. Do this for as long as it takes to feel better. Then you can look around the place and situation in which you find yourself, and find things even there that you can feel good about. You can feel good about the fact that the room you find yourself in is nice and toasty. You can feel good about sitting in a comfortable chair, etc.

> Create good feelings through a change in your attention.

It's also possible to put yourself in imaginary situations that cause you good feelings. The only proviso here is that you have to be careful not to let these imaginings lead to an underlying longing or sense of inadequacy. When you create feel-good situations in your mind, be sure that they contain enough childlike naïveté and joy so that the feeling, while thoughtful, is purely positive.

For example, say I'm alone and poor and want to be able to imagine a relationship and wealth. If I'm melancholy at the same time, the emotions that result when I try to use my imagination do not feel good.

Change the situation in your mind so that it brings on a smile. Imagine that you're an elf-princess or the king of the sprites and that you have a wealth of castles grown from plants and that you have the most amazing relationship with a fairy prince or lady sprite or whatever. Now you've visualized both relationship and wealth, and you've had fun while you were about it, without imagining any insufficiencies. When this feeling of joy has set root in this image and you can call it up quickly and easily, then you can bring it bit by bit closer to the reality you really wish for. Leave the fairy wings out at first, perhaps, but imagine yourself living in the plant castle – or vice versa: let the castle assume the form of your true dream house, while you've still got wings. Pay attention that you keep the good feeling when you change the image. It doesn't do you any harm to change the image, *unless* you keep connecting melancholy, worried feelings of insufficiency with it. If you do, the body of feeling thinks: 'Hey, this imagined situation is obviously doing you nooo good. You have to keep that man or woman far away …' Your body of feeling watches lovingly over you. And because it does, it keeps all situations that give you a bad feeling when you think about them away from you.

When you instead constantly visualize a fairy reality in a good mood, then your feelings think: 'Aha, so, wealth and relationships do us good. I really must create more of that. But what do I do about that stuff with the fairy wings? I should probably just forget about that and make sure that I get as close to this inner image as I can.'

It could happen that you find yourself, if you wished for a house, eventually in a house covered in ivy – a detail you could have done without. But isn't that better than if you had visualized a more 'reality-based' image and stayed stuck in a cramped flat that you don't like at all?! Better wealth with ivy thanks to a bit of self-circumvention.

It's just the same with money: if you always have bad feelings while spending or making money, your feelings watch over you and keep that 'bad money' away from you. It's sensible, then, to take money with a sense of gratitude and spend it with joy, and to enjoy others' success in making money. (I've written more about this in my book, *Cosmic Ordering for Beginners*.)

Your feelings watch over you. And because they do, they keep all situations away from you which give you a bad feeling when you think about them.

Approach all problems with a positive mood. With this mood and new vibration, you can find a more vibrant solution.

Einstein knew that we can never solve problems on the level they were created, and that all nature seeks harmony. Take care that nature can work within you, and relax!

What Do I Really Want?

A few years ago, I (Manfred) did a professional seminar on vision management. At the time I was surprised by the many spiritual subjects talked about in this seminar. At the end of the seminar we were asked to draw a picture of our vision and load it with a lot of feeling and energy. And it really worked! I still have the picture today. Most interesting of all was that on the way to my vision there were different tasks to wander through. I first had to make a list of what was good and what was bad in my life, and what might be a problem for me. Afterwards, I was asked whether my problems might have good sides. A lot of amazing discoveries were made that day: for example, I had the impression that some of my problems were perhaps just an excuse not to judge certain things or even approach them in any way. I could hide behind my problems and still be 'a victim of my circumstances'. My problems provided me with a lot of excuses to stay the way I'd always been.

For me, this was joined to a feeling of powerlessness and a big 'Hey, you won't succeed anyway!' At some

point I was used to this feeling of being unfulfilled and didn't believe in myself to trust in my wishes. I was conditioned not to get what I wanted, because I wanted to spare myself the disappointment and didn't even want to attempt wishing again. The spark had gone out in me to feel when I wanted something. I had somehow become hopeless. That's why it was so hard for me to recognize my wishes in that seminar; I had to learn all over again from scratch.

There was a good question asked in this seminar: What is it that I *can't* imagine at all? Climbing the Himalayas, sailing round the world, being free as a bird? And then at some point, the penny dropped: these were all subconscious things slumbering inside me as undeclared wishes! Only now they were buried so deep that, without the trick of this indirect, negative question they would never have come to light! So, a helpful trick in the search for 'What do I really want?' can be 'What *don't* I want?' in order to get its opposite.

If the wish is then clear, it still needs energy. I drew a picture for this purpose in the visions seminar. A good question to increase the energy behind a wish is the simple question: 'Why do I want it?' It's good to do this with a partner who constantly asks this question until there's an image before your inner eye which is full of joy and good energy: I really want *that* in my life because … Then there's no more room for doubt; there's a lot of joy and then the power of the heart's desire is integrated in the wish. A wish that doesn't come from the heart is not connected enough with our feeling, and our soul then thinks, 'Hey, what am I supposed to do with *that*?'

Dieter, the trainer who leads Barbel's 'Zest for Life' seminar, puts the following question to people in an exercise: 'What is the wish behind your wish?' That is, what is the reason for wanting a great car, success, relationship, recognition etc.? When this feeling is known, it's also clearer what we really want, and then we no longer have to chase after extraneous things which cannot in the end satisfy the deeper-lying feeling.

We don't often admit our real wishes to ourselves. We present problems and excuses in order not to have to trust in our 'dangerous' wishes.

Asking yourself 'Why do I want that?' or 'What can I not imagine at all?' or 'What feeling do I want when I wish for this?' gets you closer to yourself and your heart's desire.

The Voice of the Heart

We are connected to our core and our innermost being through our feelings. The fact that it is sometimes so hard for us to recognize a wish most certainly has a lot to do with the fact that we've distanced ourselves quite a bit from our innermost being. We have forgotten how to follow the voice of our heart. And by doing that, we've closed the door to the cosmos, or at best left it only a bit ajar. Working with feelings and listening increasingly to our feelings is the best way to happiness. Only in this way can we hear our inner voice even more and even better.

This distance from our feelings isn't just a problem for each of us individually; it's also a general problem in our society. As we've written at the beginning of this book, we are fed up with the over-importance of the mind in society. This rather superficial collecting of knowledge and information, as well as its rapid dissemination, has existed for a long time. A prime modern example, of course, is the Internet. There's never been a time when so much knowledge and so much information have been accessible. Our modern times also prize the rational understanding of the world, but where is the depth? Why do we need all these distractions?

More and more, however, there appear to be people who desire more real perception and experiences and, following that, those who want to allow their emotions to express themselves and develop.

These perceptions automatically further us in the search for ourselves and also for meaning in life. And besides this, they make it even more clear to us who we really are: the creators of our own universe!

Learning to feel brings us closer to our creative power all the time. And every attempt at this should be undertaken lightly, so that it's fun and we're motivated to stick with it. This is how acquiring feelings in daily life begins: ask yourself 'How do I feel physically? Am I hungry, thirsty, tired? What are my needs? What do I want to do? What makes me happy?' Often, we're so tense due to our many responsibilities that we find it hard to make room for ourselves. The idea of making a date with yourself and spending one evening a week by yourself can open entirely new doors.

When I ask myself 'How am I?' a refined perception soon emerges. And this leads to the question: 'How did this or that feel to me? Is it right for me? Should I do this or that?' It's very much a matter of talking about your feelings and expressing your feelings: '*This* is how I feel about it! This feels right or wrong to me!' We then learn to perceive things and people far differently, to strengthen our intuition muscle, and learn always to follow it and trust it more.

Apart from this, the ability to perceive and express our feelings improves, as do our partnerships and social relationships. As the magazine *Wirbelwind* (*Whirlwind*) wrote in its 'Papaextra' issue: 'Partnerships need tending: there is no way round developing a differentiated self-perception through practice. Only those who learn to identify their feelings and give them a name can say that they are enhancing their relationship.' The magazine especially recommends that men join men's groups, as it is often easier to begin sharing feelings that way than in mixed groups or with partners. Manfred initiates such men's groups and always reaches this conclusion: exercising self-perception is often easier for men when they're amongst other men!

When you begin to pay more attention to your feelings, all sorts of things will change. We have, for example, colourful walls in our house, each room a different colour, because, for us at least, it feels more cosy. We drink energized water, because it feels and tastes better, and we've used a lot of wood in the house, because we both like the smell and look of wood. We looked for a family doctor (or rather a family healer) who felt right to us, and a dentist whom we felt good with. All these things depend on the time and the place and will be different for each person. Only one thing is for sure: you will move away from the norm concerning many areas of your life, and you will move towards greater individuality. And also for each individual, the arrangement of the details of life will be completely different and feel completely different. Because everyone feels good with different things, and that's the way it's meant to be. It would be boring if everyone had the same taste. Rome would be the same as Rio de Janeiro – how boring!

EXERCISE 1

A person who doesn't recognize his feelings naturally can't communicate them.

Imagine that you're sitting in a public toilet and have forgotten to lock the door. Your most hated co-worker, or whoever makes you most uncomfortable, comes in.

How do you feel? Observe your emotions honestly.

Then imagine other people whom you wouldn't want opening the door (let's now assume the lock's broken): your mother, your father, siblings, best friend, partner, a stranger, neighbour, your child if you have one or any child if you don't, a pop star, a person whom you fear or have a lot of respect for, a person you're at odds with. Take as many possible different people and imagine them all running into the bathroom. Observe how each makes you feel. Your toddler bursting in would no doubt make you feel quite differently than if the prime minister were to walk in!.

Observe and learn your feelings to learn about yourself.

To rid yourself of this uncomfortable feeling, just imagine that you're finished, leave, and two hours later have to use the toilet again. You instinctively run to the same toilet as before, and, hey! Who's sitting there? The exact person whom it was so embarrassing to see when they came in as you were sitting there. 'Oh, now we're even,' you could say with a superior laugh and then close the door again. Observe your feeling. What is it really? What do you have to say or what do you have to do so that you feel relaxed with this situation again? Imagine the optimum solution and – very important – feel it with an open heart and with your whole spirit.

EXERCISE 2

Imagine that a Hawaiian tribe has elected you to be king or queen. This tribe consists almost solely of people who are very similar in their way of being, and because the entire tribe has spontaneously fallen in love with you, they've made you king or queen. It's a very wealthy tribe and you've automatically inherited great wealth. They've built you a sensational throne and, sitting on it, you welcome many tourists who offer you lots of money for tours of the most beautiful areas of the island. You sit on your throne now, fawned over and fanned by many servants and are bathed in love and affection by the entire tribe.

And who appears before your throne? The whole row of people with whom you've had problems in your life before: people you were afraid of, you didn't feel appreciated by, or also nice people whom you inflated and worshipped.

Observe your feelings. How do you feel now that these people are laying flowers and presents at your feet? Imagine again your family, children, partner and friends too. How would you feel with each individual person and what would you say to each? Always observe your feelings and really take note of them.

Through such exercises you get closer to yourself, get to know yourself better, become more authentic and, because of this, automatically draw more people who suit you into your life.

The acquisition of feelings starts in daily life. Ask yourself, 'How do I feel physically? Am I hungry, thirsty, tired? What are my needs? What do I want to do? What makes me happy?'

When I ask myself, 'How am I?' a refined perception soon emerges. And this leads to the question: 'How did this or that feel to me? Is it right for me? Should I do this or that?'

☆ **Part II** ☆

Feelings Produce Thoughts

Feelings in the Unconscious

Working with positive thinking is an important way for us to escape negative sticking-points and to increase our vibrations. We've already given a few examples of this earlier in this book. Part of the process of instant cosmic ordering is the acceptance that we have, to an extent, to fight with our weaker self, namely the ego, which is attracted to the negative and is judgemental and just doesn't want to grow. One way to approach this issue is to consider our personal happiness. Alongside this we need to work with our feelings.

Feelings are important in instant cosmic ordering because, even when we master the art of thinking positively, there's still a part of us that produces uncomfortable feelings, and this part is our unconscious. As valuable as positive thinking is, a danger still exists, just as with using antibiotics as a cure-all, that eventually it won't work any more. When antibiotics are used too often, bacteria strains become ever more resistant. This just shows us that everything has a natural limit. There is no panacea or miracle drug.

With positive thinking there's a danger that you might assume that you can get rid of *all* your uncomfortable feelings. We learned in Part I that everything we reject is strengthened, and that we give rejected feelings more power by rejecting them. You can also say that simply by trying to reject them, certain negative and painful feelings produce even more of themselves. They aren't healed, they're kept under lock. Think of the turf.

So what can you do? Positive thinking works with the mind and so only reaches our unconscious in a limited way. Thoughts and feelings are connected, but feelings are also self-sufficient. They can sometimes be stimulated by thoughts, but as they are the entryway to our source and the door to the cosmos, it would be surprising if they were fully and completely subordinate to our mind, wouldn't it?

The idea that feelings hide in the unconscious can at first sound like a conundrum. How can we access them there? Luckily, feelings have a life of their own; they follow a certain goal and are steered in our unconscious by our spirit. When you feel a certain feeling consistently, this is your spirit trying to help you to be emotionally 'whole' – basically, to heal. Because when a feeling is constantly pushed away and denied, we remain emotionally incomplete and can't call on our full potential. When we recognize what potential some people have to heal themselves and others, we slowly begin to understand what power might be slumbering within ourselves. Science has already proven that we only really utilize a small part of our brain. We are a lot more than we think we are, and the best path leads to recognizing our potential more fully.

Working on this book has made us even more aware of what an emotionally bad state our world is in at the moment. For this reason, we want first to put the word 'feeling' under the microscope. This may seems a bit nitpicky, but we would like to differentiate here between *feeling* and *perception*. If we want to empathize with our quint-essential heart's desire, the most important thing is the question: 'What do I really want?' And to answer this, we need a clear feeling. Then our wish, our cosmic order, has power.

A wish from the heart comes from within ourselves, from our deepest soul. It emanates from deep inside us. Perception, on the other hand, is something totally connected to yourself. Your heart gives you an answer when you ask it a question, and then you consciously perceive this answer. And this answer will be very individual, as we're all special people with our own lives and therefore our own special wishes.

What happens, though, when you ask yourself: 'What do I want?' Does an answer come that is really about you? Perhaps you want to be thinner or more attractive, because you think that if the world is more interested in you, you'll be better accepted by your partner, friends and at work? Perhaps you want more money, a great car, status, power and so on for the same reason? When, for example, you wish for a partner, do you want this partner to like

you for who you are, or for your looks, money, status …?
I don't think anyone's really free of wanting to be 'a star',
to be worthy of love. But what happens then when you
become older and feel less attractive? Cosmetic surgeons
are in high demand at the moment. Or when you lose your
status or money?

What we are getting at here are self-worth and self-
love. Of course you dress well if you love yourself, because you're worth it! And, naturally, you'll attract a partner and people in general who correspond to this feeling
of self-worth. Automatically, just magically. That's the
law of attraction. Of course, you have to know yourself.
And loving yourself also means accepting yourself just
the way you are. And that's why you should strive to
know yourself. Above all, the master question addresses
this: 'What do I really want?' And the answer can only be
felt, found in yourself.

> In order to make a wish from the heart, the first step is
> to really feel the wish within yourself.

Your heart's wish has power because you're the one who
wants it. So it would certainly be wise to know what you
like, what you perceive. You find yourself through sense,
and perhaps a lot of wishes aren't granted because you've
distanced yourself too far from your true self.

Or perhaps we sense ourselves too seldom. Sensation means that we find our source, our connection to

the universe in ourselves. Safi Nidiaye (*Herz öffnen statt Kopf zerbrechen*), who has done a lot of work on the heart and feelings, brings it all to a point with the words she has gained from her own experience: trusting yourself to sense with your heart is 'to really love yourself for the first time'. Perhaps it is here, in sensation, that life really first begins. And this is why exercises in perception and sensing are very important elements in Barbel's 'Zest for Life' seminars.

Specifically, we must be consistent and always use the term 'to sense' when it has to do with the perception that takes place from an open heart. This might not work in every case in this book (in the chapter 'Thoughts Create Feelings and Feelings Create Thoughts' we called it heart-feelings, because we hadn't explained the term yet), as 'to feel' and 'to sense' can often get jumbled up. And really, practically, we only rarely properly 'sense' in our daily lives. Because to sense requires discipline, focusing the mind on the perception, the sensation, and becoming aware of the perception from within. And so, unfortunately, we only feel in 'snapshots'. We hope with this book to contribute to helping you succeed increasingly and more fully in sensing and perception.

Our normal condition, unfortunately, is to lack this feeling from the heart more often than not. In normal life we function rather automatically and don't usually ask ourselves what we're feeling at any given moment, nor what would do us good right about now. In this rather unconscious, automatic mode, we forget to feel and so sense less of ourselves and a lot more of our surroundings. We follow the responsibilities of our job and the everyday more than our heart. We lose ourselves in thought, and concern ourselves with problems from yesterday and tomorrow. At the same time, naturally, we feel less of the present and only a little of ourselves.

When our thoughts occupy themselves with yesterday and tomorrow, we also produce feelings: perhaps we constantly dwell on situations from the past. Our ego plays a trick on us and in doing so attaches itself to the feelings identified with the past. We stay stuck in the feeling and are somehow in thrall to it. We already know that the ego loves to speak and think negatively. Negative feelings give the ego amazing energy. These feelings rob us of power and demoralize us.

By contrast, experience is free from association with the past. Experience is only fleeting and always new, always in the now. Experience is free from sorrow because it connects us with the source of our being, enriches us and makes us creative. To experience also means to be grounded – and that's what the next chapter is about.

When a feeling is constantly pushed away or denied, we remain emotionally incomplete and can't call on our full potential.

The word experience means 'to find something within yourself'. With experience, you find something inside that is totally connected to you.

In order to make a wish from the heart, the first step is to feel the wish and find the place inside you that corresponds to it. Your heart's desire has power because you're truly yourself in wanting it.

Feelings Want to Be Born

Experience brings us back, then, to the ego. The ego evaluates, judges and calculates, makes itself good and others bad. It criticizes and demands perfection, and loves most to complain about mistakes and insufficiencies in itself as well as others. So the ego *doesn't* experience the other, as would happen with feeling, but excludes, bounces the other away and a fight starts, a competition, for who is better, who is right and so on.

> The ego sees only itself; it can't really sense or feel. Only the sympathetic heart can really feel. So the way into the heart and into feelings always involves a fight with the ego.

One can also say that the more the ego refines itself, the more it becomes open to experience. The head and the ego stand on one side, the heart and experience on the other. And the 'truth' of the ego can be very different from the 'truth' of the heart.

A friend of ours had a kind of near-death experience in which the ego and the head wanted to go in one direction and her heart and experience in another. Peaceful again and in a trance in her heart, she asked, very clearly, and saw that the near-death experience was comfortable and not at all horrible. Similar death experiences have been documented by Elisabeth Kübler-Ross. There absolutely is a difference between 'the truth of the heart' and 'the truth of the head'. I suppose that, indeed, the theory belonging to the study of neuro-linguistic programming (NLP) – that you can influence and create feelings with thoughts – is correct. But the fact that the head can influence only the feeling, not the experience, shows that it's only when the head is at peace and our judgemental, critical side is sleeping that we can hear the quiet voice of the heart.

All of us are connected to one another through our emotional bodies. Every person is, then, part of one overall emotional body. It is through this body that phenomena such as 'remote viewing' and clairvoyance take place. When the heart is open and experience occurs, then a person can really empathize, exactly in the same way he or she can feel and perceive him- or herself. If the heart's not open, this contact takes place not with the heart, but with the mind and is full of judgement and criticism, and this 'feeling' is not coming from our innermost spirit.

As already described, Carl Jung found a good definition to differentiate between experience and feeling: experience comes first. It is the original, then comes thought and only then, feeling. In this chain, the feeling values what experience has first assessed free of judgement. Experience is therefore without criticism or value judgements, so still free of the ego. The ego only comes after and then decides on the way, through thought, of how it wants to approach what's happened. So, the ego *decides* what it *wants* to feel!

> It may seem hard to believe, but we decide (mostly unconsciously) how we feel. We ourselves decide if we're victims or if we want to use our power to become ever clearer and give up the role of victim.

As with a radio, the ego decides which station we want to tune into. That is, what we want to hear. But we have free choice of all the frequencies of feelings. The ego, of course, wants to make itself important and likes to choose the 'self-pity' or 'delusions of grandeur' station. But the more we refine the ego, the more these stations no longer please us and the more seldom we select these emotional frequencies.

If the heart is closed, then certain negative feelings cannot be brought to life as the ego has too strong a grip on you. The ego just doesn't want to grow. And then it's as if a blockage exists, the feelings pile up and create pressure. Because the feelings wish to be born. The spirit continually creates new situations that keep repeating themselves until this certain feeling can be brought to life. This is why the same type of man always comes into the life of a certain woman, and why similar family situations or certain work environments replay themselves over and over. Pushing away these feelings makes them stronger.

Once again (but this is really the last time), we want to use the fear of being bitten by a dog as an example. At the time I was bitten, I was still too young to be able to judge the situation emotionally, and internally 'checked out' of the scenario. I separated my experience from reality and thus avoided facing up to the situation. Unfortunately, I have certainly not avoided the physically uncomfortable feeling of 'being bitten by a dog' and therefore haven't been able to integrate it into my life and have somehow energetically blocked it. Now I'm unconsciously looking for a situation where this experience can be reactivated so that I can feel it and integrate it into my life. The energy block will be removed in this way.

In psychology, one uses the term 'personality disorder' for profound problems that occurred in childhood and couldn't be coped with. People with these problems constantly pull similar instances into their later life, repeating certain patterns over and over. What at first seems to be absurd or stupid behaviour can be seen as a psychological dysfunction, though in terms of feelings it makes sense: the continually repeated uncomfortable experiences are connected to suppressed and blocked feelings, which finally want to be to be experienced and resolved.

Feelings want to be born. Another way of looking at this would be to examine the phenomenon that the spirit seeks out certain themes before incarnation, perhaps from past lives, in order to live them out in the next life and be transformed. If feelings are denied, then they aren't born and are stuck somewhere travelling between heaven and hell (if you will). Considered further, a person who doesn't really feel is in a way not really born. This leads us again to the point that all of us know only a minute part of our potential. because, from the point of view of experience, none of us is truly, fully alive. Coming to terms with feeling and unknown pain is therefore a very good way to be, one could even say a good way to be whole. For this reason, the Sufis have blessed everyone from ancient times on with the words: 'Be that which you always are!' – which means feeling with an open heart – and with that, to someday fulfil your highest potential.

A coarse, unrefined ego can't take criticism. It disturbs the process of creation by seeking perfectionism always. It isn't one with everything, but puts all its power in separation.

Whoever can really feel what is, in themselves and around them, and who can always give love precedence – that is, whoever can love their failures and allow others to become better than they are – holds the real power of creation in their hands. A refined ego is closer to universal Oneness. It frees itself of its fixation on separation, and so receives entry to the creative energy of Oneness.

Being able to feel with pleasure and depth, a lot of self-loving and a refined ego = a lot of creativity.

Low self-esteem, a coarse ego, seeing 'sentimentality' as uncool = little creativity.

Different Types of Feeling

In many regions of the world, there are different terms for snow in order to describe precisely its variations. In our culture there are no fewer than 125 different grey tones in the colour scale …

That's just a little joke. But what we could probably use more than 125 grey tones are more clear, distinguishable terms in the feelings sector. We have only one term for many different things. This leads to confusion. Due to this, we can hardly communicate what we're feeling at any moment, because we lack the words to describe it. So we're always trying to differentiate and to somehow define what we're feeling with the terms that are at hand. In this chapter we'd like to introduce a few subdivisions and to illuminate them more exactly. Because even thinking about how we express ourselves has an 'ordering' effect on feelings. The words we use don't really matter in the end, it's just about becoming more knowledgeable, within ourselves, about the different types of feelings.

1. Feeling in the Now

We use the word *feeling* for sensations we experience in an instant. Carl Jung would call this the first *experience*, the first sensing of our surroundings. (Remember, it isn't about which term you use, but just choosing one you can use to express the idea of an emotion's true source.)

If we consistently distinguish a feeling in the now from other kinds of feelings, we improve the fineness of our perception as well as our understanding of ourselves. And then, later, we can forget all of the different terms and use the word *feeling* as an umbrella term. Because if we get caught up in over-thinking about which term is correct, then we're guaranteed to be in our heads and not in our hearts.

Example 1: My dog is run over, I experience a feeling of grief. This is normal, healthy and belongs to the moment.

2. Emotion

The word 'emotion' comes from the Latin *ex*, 'out of', and *motio*, 'movement, excitement'. When a feeling arising instantaneously is too severe and the person who has the feeling cannot deal with it at the time, it becomes suppressed instead of experienced. This feeling is then stored in the cells. Thus, when an old feeling boils up from below because it wants to be seen and released, it can seem to have little to do with what's happening in the current moment.

Example 2: My dog was run over when I was a child. I was told that I shouldn't cry and the unexpressed feeling has stored itself away at the bodily level and has become an emotion. Whenever someone near me becomes highly emotional, it makes me uncomfortable. I 'feel' queasy, because the other person's radiance awakens the old emotions in me. I don't want this, thus I must fend off the attack as soon as possible, for example by reacting coldly.

3. Intuitive Feeling

The word 'intuitive' again comes from the Latin, this time the word *intueor* meaning 'to examine, deliberate'. Another term for this type of feeling might also be a 'gut feeling'. As we've mentioned earlier in this book, some feelings are like compressed thoughts that are then stored away. They sum up our experiences and thus allow us quicker access to stored-away data. So, when we are faced with a complicated situation, we usually don't have to process each factor in our heads individually, rather, a kind of whole feeling tells us what's up.

Example 3: I want to hire a new cleaning lady and have three to choose from. Without having to study each factor such as voice, posture, eye contact, facial expression and aura, a kind of entire feeling tells me which person is best.

This we've chosen to call intuitive feeling. This feeling is a kind of summarized overall impression based on your past experience of life. Intuition is not infallible, though, because it relies not just upon your experience of life but also your current assessments of the world, and these can be at least partially ill-founded or misleading.

4. The Seventh Sense

This is a special form of feeling for which we have invented the term 'seventh sense' – though you'll probably recognize and understand the concept behind it already. The seventh sense describes the kind of inner sensitivity possessed only by those people who have achieved a more objective, higher perspective, beyond the demands of their ego and not limited by their past experiences.

5. Experience

True experience is found in the peace of your own open heart. You can find a totally private, fulfilling sensory world there. This type of experience is in stark contrast to the experiences which originate from external sources.

Experiences can also be absorbed completely from the outside. We can feel with someone, for instance, form a connection with them, and thus 'absorb' their feeling easily, often unnoticed by our consciousness. A person can only really empathize with someone, however, if they can genuinely feel within themselves what the other person is feeling.

Feelings don't necessarily have to begin with or belong solely to me. On the contrary, if a person has a certain emptiness within, if they don't listen to their heart, don't know what is good for them, don't really live and obey only the opinions of the outside world, they fill themselves with all kinds of compensatory things, and come to assume that the feelings of the outside world around them are their own.

It's already a trend in our society that more interest is shown in the outside world than in our own, internal processes. Our internal emptiness is filled with information and 'borrowed emotions' originating from the outside world. The emptiness cannot be satisfied in this way, however. It can only be cured by looking inwards, through engaging with your feelings and fears and accepting even the unpleasant ones. In return, you will experience your own original being.

Hence, what we're calling 'experience' here is also the universal part of us that feels. Experience in this sense is the feelings of the soul. Which experience arises in you if you listen completely to the silence within? If suddenly the earth-bound ego goes silent and you listen in to the universal elemental power within yourself, if you open your heart and just *be*, without expectations and without judgement, then the experiences rise up within you which express what your soul wishes to communicate. Hence, this type of feeling, this experience, is deeply satisfying, because it reconnects us to our elemental power. We suddenly no longer feel separate from ourselves and what's around us; instead we have a feeling of oneness with everything.

The single word 'feeling', therefore, is a bad fit because it cannot accurately describe this experience of the universal-divine unity, which is not a feeling originating in the moment but is the elemental feeling which is, in fact, always in us (we're usually just too preoccupied with everyday worries and concerns to perceive it). However, the more often we explore this experience, the more our 'life-batteries', our internal strength, are boosted, and we take a simple joy in everything we do. Experiencing yourself and your own universal-divine core results in a fulfilling feeling of wholeness and blithe, self-sufficient contentment. We float internally, connected to a living manifestation of the oneness of all. We can also describe this experience as the 'feeling of the Oneness in ourselves'.

Now, this experience also wants to be felt and wants to express itself. It's the feeling with the most creativity, from a spiritual point of view. If an experience comes directly from the core of your spirit and is allowed to flow freely, and is recognized as such, it comes into being quickly. The more a person cuts himself off from it, the more this person and his soul feel homeless. He no longer has a home within himself and no longer really senses himself. This means that he is removed from the experience of his own creativity. Instead, compensatory feelings are created, slowly and more tenaciously. This means that things happen to the soul which it doesn't feel and therefore doesn't understand.

For example: Let's say that your soul wants to experience connection with another. However, you are so removed from being able to acknowledge this, in part because it is so tied up with your fear of being alone, that you spend your time drinking with friends in order to feel accepted. The fear of separation and rejection makes you overlook others who would, in fact, answer what your soul wants, and instead you spend your time with people who don't, and you try compulsively to adapt to this. And the more you 'adapt' in this way, the more out of touch you get with what your soul truly understands. You are cut off from your experience, your source. Out of your own inner emptiness, you search for corresponding feelings in your surroundings, and busy yourself round the clock with feelings which originate *outside* yourself. In the end, you become almost addicted to externalizing your feelings. This does provide a kind of comfort zone, but it is false, because what you are actually searching for is a return to the experience of your source.

Feeling originates in the moment.

Emotions are feelings not yet fully experienced and stored away deep inside.

Intuitive feeling summarizes impressions and compares them to existing experiences.

Our seventh sense describes an inner sensitivity possessed only by those people who have achieved a higher perspective.

Experience is the feeling of oneness in us. It comes from the heart and from our soul and has the most creative power. All wishes that originate from our true experience have the best chance of coming true.

Every Feeling Contains Its Opposite

Visible laws that are valid in the material world are also valid in the invisible world. This will make clear to us the following statement, dating back to the Middle Ages: 'As above, so below.' What is obviously true of the visible, material world, is also true invisibly, in the spiritual and emotional worlds.

When we stand on the beach, waves come and go. Even when we can't see them, they are there, beneath the surface, ebbing and flowing, peaking and troughing. It's an expression of nature's polarity, just as with light and dark. Polarity is made up of opposites which are always changing in order to find a balance.

Spiritual meaning follows the same rules. For instance, the Sufis believe that the absence of a certain quality in your life means only that you should deal more closely with this quality. If it isn't there, it is your job to get it back. This can be anything from the power of self-assertion to acceptance of sympathy and wisdom. And because the Sufis believe that everything which exists was created by God (and they certainly aren't alone in this belief), every quality and characteristic that a person can possess is also of a divine nature. Hence, they use certain invocations for God, so-called *wasifas*, to bring more of certain qualities into their lives. Wasifas are somewhat similar to mantras, or prayer. As with waves, the seeming absence of a certain trait within ourselves doesn't mean it isn't there, or that we don't possess it, but only that it is hidden and needs to be 'brought to the surface'.

The 'hermetic' philosophy used by the Sufis dates back to Hermes Trismegistus, who is said to have lived about 2,000 years before Christ. His philosophy is based on seven axioms or principles, the second of which we already know (As above, so below). Here is an overview of the Hermetic principles:

1. Mentality: all is mind, the universe is spiritual.
2. Correspondence: as above, so below; as below, so above. Laws applicable to material things also apply to the soul and mind, and vice versa.
3. Vibration: nothing rests, everything moves, everything vibrates.
4. Polarity: everything is dual, everything has a pair of opposites. Everything is and isn't at the same time. Opposites are identical by nature, yet different in degree. All paradoxes may be reconciled.
5. Rhythm: everything flows. Everything has its tides. Everything rises and falls. Rhythm equalizes.

6. Cause and effect: every cause has an effect. Every effect has a cause. Everything happens for a reason.
7. Gender: gender is in everything. Everything has male and female principles in it.

The fourth principle says that everything is built on opposites. According to the fifth principle, these opposites merge and are equalized by rhythm. It becomes clear here as well that a characteristic in a person can only exist if at the same time its opposite also exists, even if it's not yet obvious.

Heraclites, the Greek philosopher, was even more clear about this. He lived possibly around 500 years before Christ. To him, the world of human experience is also built around opposites. Summer and winter, warmth and cold, day and night, wealth and poverty – we can only know something if we also know of its corresponding opposite. Every quality is understandable only in contrast to its opposite. In addition, Heraclites recognized a 'unity of contrasts': for him, through his knowledge of *panta rhei* ('everything flows'), a static world is impossible. Only change is everlasting. The visible contrasts in the world are always merging into each other. Day turns to dusk, then to night and from dawn to day again. The wave comes and the wave goes. For Heraclites the ever-changing world is affected by a 'clash of opposites', a clash which leads in the best sense to inherent harmony, so that all polarities can alternate in our world of experience over and over again. However, for Heraclites these polarities and contrasts exist at the same time and form contrasting pairs which are inseparable, such as day/night, summer/winter. He looks at these pairs as the unity which contains both sides of itself, as in the Yin-Yang symbol. Both aspects of the entity (such as day/night) require each other: without night there would also be no day. Day and night are forever merging into each other; lose one and both are lost.

For Heraclites, each thing reveals its opposite. Each presence reveals a concealed, more deeply recumbent unity which contains the apparent opposites and brings them together again. For Heraclites 'the clash is the being of all things' which contains true harmony in itself.

Within opposites, however, one quality will be dominant. With light and dark, light is quite clearly dominant. If it is dark and we turn on the light, then it gets light. (Just try sometime to switch on the dark if it's light.) So, dark is only the absence of light. Light dominates over dark. A conciliatory aspect of duality, as it is also seen, is that love always dominates over hate. Hatred just disappears like the darkness when love awakes.

What does this mean for our feelings? If the supposition 'As above, so below' is taken to its logical conclusion, a kind of wave-effect can be accepted as part of our feelings. You can see this quite easily with teenagers, who are typically up one minute and down the next. Feelings are being developed here, just as a person grows and develops. Feelings also need balance, and so we experience the inevitable 'down time' or 'the blues' after a particularly wonderful encounter or a great weekend. This certainly shouldn't mean that we have to suffer from this oscillation. The suffering only first comes into being when we don't really want to experience certain feelings and don't accept one side of the polarity (e.g. unhappiness/joy). Then the positive side of the contrasting pair cannot come to life either.

A feeling is always connected to its opposite. If you don't allow the wave trough, you don't get the wave crest. If we learn to feel and live something that's not good, it frees the way for the positive aspect of this duality, namely that which makes us happy.

Now, because all this probably sounds very abstract, let's give you a few examples.

From my (Barbel's) own experience, I can say that if a negative feeling is really felt, it evaporates and becomes its opposite. However, this is awful for the ego. As has already been described, the ego sticks to negative feelings. If then such a feeling is resolved, the ego believes it's dying. But for all this, a little more of the true self comes to light and is born.

For me (Manfred), my life was marked early by the experience of separation. After I had my first painful big love affair at 17, a further two painful separations happened for me and were connected with long and agonizing, self-lacerating questions: 'What did I do wrong?' 'What could I have done better?' 'You'll never find a woman that great again!' etc. However, I always found distractions so as not to experience my feeling of loneliness and rejection: there were always friends with whom I could talk and talk about it, there was work, going to school, television, whatever. Then, however, something happened: I succeeded in really getting into the feeling, within myself, of experiencing rejection. And something very strange happened, unbelievable: I began to do really well! I felt loved, protected, secure quite by myself and alone. It was as if my spirit realized, 'Great! Something good is happening here! Keep going!' I explored the loneliness properly, spent a lot of time in the country, avoided ceaselessly talking the subject to death. And I somehow succeeded in becoming more dependent on myself, not needing anyone else to fill the space which opened wide when I was alone.

> An unpleasant feeling, experienced fully, converts itself into its opposite.

Love is a state of pure being that does not need to change into its opposite because it is the origin of being. Nevertheless, an opposite is also created, sometimes bigger, sometimes smaller, distancing you from the fount of all being but enabling you to perceive all the more clearly when you regain it again.

To go back to my example, only when I had learned to be with myself could I find Barbel, a woman who wanted children with me! Hey, this was new! And all at once I could also say what I wanted in the relationship and for myself, whereas before, due to the fear of separation or rejection, I did everything I could not to be alone – and drove others away in the process!

> If you don't love yourself, you can only love others badly.

In any case, I'm sure that because I have experienced separation, I don't need to fear it any more in my life. It has been experienced and resolved. My 'fear of the fear' of separation is gone and has given way to greater self-confidence. I know I can live through the loneliness of separation, because I have been allowed to find out the positive side of it and with this my soul has moved forward, so there's no reason for me to fear it any longer.

> If we say 'Yes' to life instead of 'No', we remove all opposition.

We can say 'Yes' to any experience, however seemingly difficult or unhappy, and use the time to work on ourselves and prepare for the next, higher level of being. Saying 'No' to life means being stuck in old patterns. Since 'No' has a strong energy, it holds us firmly in rejection. Only acceptance resolves the connection and frees the way for a new relationship or new, positive life experiences at a higher level. In the case of relationships, most people know that you meet the right one when you've stopped looking. When you let go and are genuinely happy to work on yourself, any relationship you encounter while you're in this energetic state will have a lot going for it.

The Feeling Heart: Jewish Kabbalah

As is so often the case with what seems new to us, the knowledge of feelings and experience is as old as humanity. However, what is new is that this knowledge is now available to all. However, knowledge alone isn't enough; energy is required to bring this knowledge to life.

In other words, the idea of a new aim is one thing, but it needs activation, namely the right feeling, so that this aim can really come into being. As mentioned earlier in this book, feelings are our 'emotional navigation system': they want to show us whether we are headed towards our desired target or away from it.

With every moment in which we have a negative feeling, we move away from our goal.

With every moment in which we have a positive feeling, we get closer to our goal.

So our most important task when creating our desired reality is to be sure that we have predominantly positive feelings. If we manage this, life also allows us the opportunity to reach exactly what we've ordered, dreamed or wished. And to have deeply felt positive feelings, we must make friends first with the old feelings stored away within us.

We are of the opinion that many more books will be written about feelings in the next few years, and that lots of old knowledge will be discovered anew. Because we have moved so far from our feelings, as a society, the trip back to them will take a while.

The knowledge of feelings is inscribed in the codes of the ancient Jewish mystical school of Kabbalah. The Kabbalah shows the way for each of us to reach perfect existence. It is described by ten different qualities called *Sephirot*, and each of these qualities shows a step towards spiritual growth. As a person develops, he deals with one of these steps, studying the writings that go with it. Depending on a person's development, he experiences these developmental steps either in the light or the dark. Because the Sephirot, like the Hermetic principles, are made up of opposites. For instance, the eighth Sephirah has the name splendour and/or grief, depending on a person's advancement. The sixth Sephirah, called Tipheret, is connected with compassion, love and acceptance, but also with criticism and perfectionism (those aspects associated with the human ego).

On the way through the various levels of the Kabbalah, on the path to wisdom, this step of opening your heart (the sixth Sephirah) is essential if you are to progress further. The levels and gifts of the other Sephirot remain closed to the person who cannot open his heart.

The seventh level stands for intuition and clairvoyance, the eighth level for power (thoughts, creative strength and also wishes), and the ninth level for wisdom and integrity in the form of connection with all people, the oneness with all. The sixth Sephirah is 'the door to the heart'. Whoever strides through this door becomes open to the beauty of this world and develops real empathy and sympathy. And an open heart is the key to instant cosmic ordering.

For example, Manfred and I were once in a foreign airport looking for our departure gate. Suddenly Manfred had disappeared, along with the baggage and tickets. I couldn't see him anywhere. Just what I needed. I was already stressed anyway. Just one more thing in this stressful situation and I would begin to panic. Then I remembered that the feeling of stress had probably only created the problem and that it was, therefore, about time I returned to myself, to breathe deeply and to go back to the feeling of trust.

This isn't, of course, easy in such a moment. But I simply stopped, took a deep breath, closed my eyes for one moment, remembered some moment of trust in my life and tried to observe the feeling in my body: 'How does it feel again when I put myself fully into a feeling of trust? How was that? Oh yes, kind of like this.' And with the thought: 'If I don't find him on time through trust, then without trust surely not,' I opened my eyes and saw Manfred immediately and how he was standing there looking at me.

And we made the flight.

> What was early secret knowledge is today accessible to everybody: namely, that the mind is there to make decisions, and feelings are our navigation system.
>
> Good feelings coming from the heart signal that you are on the right path. Small doubts signal small detours; large doubts, fear and worries are a sign that you are moving in the opposite direction from your purpose.

When Experience Has Lost Its Way

Let's come back to experience and the way to discovering it anew. But let's start from the beginning: with the mind and what consequences it has when we, as so often in our hectic lives, are rather cut off from experience. We don't sense ourselves, are always running away from ourselves. Translated into daily life, this happens in various ways. The balance of our surroundings with feelings can be experienced in the infectious excitement of a fan for a football club, a parent with a child, a partner with a partner, in reading about the lives of our stars or idols, or despairing for the world because of all the negative news and disasters that befall it. This list can be continued *ad infinitum*. The never-ending stream of impressions (not least from the ever-expanding Internet) shows the pace and scale at which we have moved away from our own feelings and are falling back on outside feelings to compensate.

For myself (Manfred) there is a whole list of possibilities which I use repeatedly to cut myself off from feeling: television, the Internet, video games, DVDs, reading, appointments, eating badly, not taking care of my body, dwelling on the past, whining and complaining, enjoying the negative. From my point of view, all forms of 'entertainment' which I can't really control are basically addictions that lead me to destroy my own energy and not utilize it where it would do me good: in the now.

Opening Up to Sensitivity

We saw a play called *African Footstep* last year (2006) at the Deutsche Theatre in Munich. The show was very well done and I (Barbel) also liked the music very much. At least, part of me did. Unfortunately, the volume was set for those used to too much chatting on the mobile, already acoustically nerve-fried and half-deaf. I had to ball up tissue and put it in my ears, because they were really aching. With stopped-up ears, it all was going well. Or so I thought.

I thought about this again a few weeks later when I was on holiday in Verona and attended a production of *Madame Butterfly* by Puccini. The difference was absolutely amazing. The Arena di Verona is a gigantic Roman amphitheatre, like the Coliseum in Rome, for audiences of up to 15,000. The acoustics in the arena are excellent – so much so that even today they do not use a loudspeaker during the performance.

The audience was asked at the beginning of the performance not to rustle paper and also to be quiet, because every noise disturbs the enjoyment of the music. And this is true. Because neither the orchestra nor the singers are amplified by technology, but are heard purely, every other noise really interferes. The result was that every cell of my being was wide open to absorbing the silence and the sounds of the arena (we were sitting quite far from the stage, right up in the cheap seats). With the warm summer air and the starry sky around us, the feeling produced was totally meditative and wonderful. And at some point, the atmosphere at the Deutsche Theatre occurred to me in contrast.

At that time, indeed, the tissues in my ears made them stop aching, but the cells of my body were not wide open and – I only realized this once I was in the Arena di Verona – I had a feeling of strain and alarm. The music at *African Footstep* was so loud that my whole body quaked and had vibrated with it. And it didn't like it. I left the performance happy about the melodies, and yet somehow exhausted. The volume had been stressful for my whole body.

After the Arena di Verona, I felt like I do after being at a relaxing, energetically restorative and extremely spiritual wellness treatment. And I had the feeling that in such a place there is room for experience (found in itself).

The experience awakens when it becomes bored with purely compensatory feelings: in the easy, simple, the quiet, slow. In all these qualities is room where I can find myself in myself, where I can listen to my feelings and they aren't drowned out. And this is exactly what I like to do in order to give experience room within me: to keep a lookout for quiet things and places, to open up an inner room for myself in which I feel free and unhindered, and can experience. Power comes directly to me here: in the silence and in the moments when I can open up confidently to pay attention to the finest perception in myself and enjoy it.

On the subject of sensitivity, which we all possess even if we mostly underestimate it, I would like to add another two small examples. Natural oils and artificial oils in perfume have quite different radiances. They smell differently and our body reacts differently to them. Artificial oils are produced in a lab, so the smell isn't the same as that produced by nature. The body enjoys the natural oil more intensively. As in the Arena di Verona, the body's cells tend to open up more and take the smell in more fully. Natural smells cause many varied reactions in the body of feelings as well. With artificial smells, the perception is much more superficial and 'disappoints the nose'. That 'something' that it's looking for can't be found.

The second example comes from Core Quantum Method (CQM) seminars (www.hypervoyager.de). CQM explains, among other things, that we sense and experience far more things than we are usually aware of. An exercise that demonstrates this is called 'Stop-and-Go'. The exercise is done in pairs. One person sits on a chair and says aloud either 'stop' or 'go' and the person either stops or goes. At some point, the person in the chair stops speaking aloud and only thinks the commands. The other person has the task of sensing the commands and reacting to them. The better the basic feeling of wellbeing in the group, the more everyone feels connected and happily animated, the better the exercise works and it can be a very exciting experience. Each of us can feel 'something in the air', but we must look inside, or rather sense inside, or 'hyper-sense' it. We all have these instincts and they are astonishingly exact. If we want to train our perception and sensitivity, we must consciously keep a lookout for such moments and opportunities. Because in an environment that's overwhelmingly loud and unnatural, the space for feelings and experience is usually missing.

And if you are alienated from your fine perception, then how can you be genuine? If you are not genuine, then how can you – according to the rules of attraction – pull into your life that which is harmonious to you and people who suit you? How can you count on your refined feelings as a navigational system through life towards the fulfilment of your heart's desire if you don't practise really noticing these feelings?

People who get to know their feelings better get to know themselves better. People who feel themselves and are genuine pull that into their lives which suits them and belongs to them.

> The person who trains their fine perception trains their 'happiness navigation system'. Follow your innermost, subtlest feelings of wellbeing and you will reach your highest potential in life!

Freeing Suppressed Feelings

If a negative feeling is really felt and experienced, it resolves itself into its opposite. This is the magic of feelings! And as astonishing as it may seem, when it comes to experience and feeling, it's about sending the mind to sleep. Away from the mind, an automatic system, your autopilot, resolves and changes the feeling. You could also say: the experienced feeling knows its way!

So 'negative' feelings have a tendency to change into their opposite when these feelings are truly experienced. That's good news: there is always a way to resolution. So feeling can be compared to a vector in physics: a feeling has power (surprise, surprise) and also a course.

Make contact with your feelings and ask, for example, in a relaxed and attentive mood: What do I feel? How do I feel? What do I need? What do you need, my pain? And – and this is a small miracle – the answer will be a body feeling, an impulse that means nothing more than that the body is working with your feelings towards a resolution, for example, of pain.

How does this work in practice? How do we locate old feelings, stored in cell memory and at some point suppressed? Let's assume you're practising the exercises from Part I of this book and have discovered that it's easier than you thought to pull up your buried feelings in small steps, piece by piece. But in some situations old feelings come up from somewhere in the depths over and over again and irritate and disturb your progress. Quite clearly, these are old patterns stored in your cell memory which become apparent because they would like to leave their cellular prison and be released.

> Feelings which at some point overwhelmed us are kept stored in the cell memory and in the organs until they are released.

But where's the key to the prison cell? That's easy: just look that locked-up cell right in the eye and it'll disappear.

You can try this exercise with any negative feeling, at the moment it appears. No matter if it's based on old patterns or is a new negative feeling, *don't follow your first impulse to look away and plaster over it, but look it right in the face:* 'Aha, got you! What brought you to the surface? Where in my body can I feel you, which reactions do you cause in me?' Look exactly at what's happening, and let nothing escape you. What does the negative feeling, which is also a kind of energy-thief, do in this situation? It becomes frightened that it's been discovered and scurries away out of your system.

Something quite similar happens with feelings of rejection. As the saying goes, 'Geese fly in flocks; eagles fly alone.' If you have ever felt rejected by the 'geese' around you (at school, at work, in any social situation), remember that you are an eagle, circling quietly bemused as you observe the silly geese. The feeling of rejection, once looked in the face and accepted, becomes empowerment.

As soon as you try to suppress a negative feeling, it becomes big and mighty. If you look at it and feel it from all sides, it slips right through your fingers and, just that quickly, it's gone.

If you suppress feelings, they are stored in your cell memory until you are ready to release them.

Stored feelings want to be released; they want to draw attention to their 'detention'.

If they are released, they stop creating reality. What doesn't exist can't create.

The Photo-album Exercise: Feeling Old Feelings to Their End

Of course, you have to practise not running away from negative feelings and painful old patterns that turn up out of the blue. If you manage to face them instead, then nothing else can hurt or frighten you for long. No sorrow will be never-ending or even continue past the natural end of a fully experienced mourning period. Sorrow that has come to a natural end leaves nothing behind but love, not sadness.

Practice is the order of the day; after all, you've spent a long time practising suppressing these feelings. The ironic thing is that what we suppress most is our connection to our own divinity, to the elemental power within us. In a panic we slam the door in the face of the cosmic delivery man. But the person who feels fully finds their way back to oneness. But what is the best way to practise?

The photo-album technique is one possibility, and perfectly suited to experiencing old stored-up feelings to their end. You don't need to wait until life creates one of those situations when old feelings come roaring to the surface; you can do some groundwork with this photo-album technique, and so both get to know your feelings better and release a lot of stored-up emotion.

When you leaf through your photo album, keep an eye out for any blockages and melancholy around each image. If you let yourself surrender to the feeling of, 'No wonder I feel as bad as I do, when my poor family have always had such a bad time,' the danger is that you are letting your ego take over, and letting it, and you, wallow in self-pity again. Your aim should be to achieve something quite different.

If, on the other hand, you haven't thoroughly examined your feelings very often before, and were brought up to confront each problem positively at any cost, then it can be exceptionally healing to let the complete opposite happen for once.

> Remember: a negative feeling is released as soon as you have felt it to its very end.

The photo-album exercise gives you a great number of first-class opportunities to sink yourself emotionally into all of your family dramas and to 'feel them to their end'.

Remember: It is important not to turn this into an ego exercise of self-pity and regret. Always focus on the fact that the essence of this exercise lies in transformation towards the light.

How to Do It
- Burn cleansing incense or essential oils.
- Play background music that is peaceful and relaxing.
- Turn down the lights or light candles.
- Make sure that you won't be disturbed (telephone, children ...).
- If you have any mascots, a statue of the Buddha or another symbol of oneness, purity or protection, set them up around you.
- Gather together family photo albums of your childhood, your parents, grandparents, ancestors etc.

This might all sound terribly kitsch, but it helps make it absolutely clear to your ego that you aren't going through the albums just to cook yourself up a psychic soup spiced with a huge pinch of self-pity. If, however, you're better able to create this feeling of transformation without any incense, candles or other paraphernalia, then that's fine, of course. Or perhaps you would prefer to do it surrounded by nature – then go for it: pack your albums in a rucksack and off you go into the countryside.

Once you're there, sitting in the centre of your circle of candles, out in the countryside or wherever, start looking at the first photos in your album.

EXERCISE 1

As you look at each photo, take time to observe each negative feeling you discover, how it travels around your body, or where you feel it most intensely. Observe it and speak to the feeling in your thoughts: 'Hello, feeling. How are you? What do you need? What can I do for you? How do you feel, feeling?' or also, 'Dear feeling, I want to feel you as intensely as possible. How can I strengthen you further?' As you're asking the questions from your position as observer, your ego won't be able to identify with the feeling so completely. And when the feeling has truly been felt to its very end, you'll experience its opposite. This means that after tragedy, happiness; that after sorrow, a smile will grow within you; and so on.

After a break-up when I (Barbel) was young, I decided not to wallow for ages in the pain, but to get through the whole process in one go. I cancelled all appointments and social arrangements for three days, drew all the curtains, surrounded myself with mountains of tissues, and sat down to have a good, long cry. It started well: I felt very tragic. I concentrated on these feelings on purpose, to experience them to their depths. I wanted to descend to the deepest valley of this sorrow in the furthest corner of my being.

What happened? After 15 minutes I had an unbelievable fit of the giggles. I laughed and laughed, at myself and at the fact that I was sitting there in my little flat with the curtains drawn. The giggles lasted for quite a long time. When this spell was over, I sat waiting for the next wave of sorrow. After all, I didn't want to leave any of it out. But nothing came. I searched and examined and dug deeply into myself, and each time ended up laughing again. I couldn't find any more. I was finished and never felt sad again about this wonderfully magic and romantic relationship that had been more important to me than anything else. That was almost two decades ago. I truly was through with it in 15 minutes.

EXERCISE 2

If the photo-album exercise has worked well, you'll now have experienced that 'behind the clouds the sun is always shining' feeling of natural joy and of oneness with life. The elemental power will well up within you after you feel a negative feeling to its very end.

Now look again at each photo that gave you negative feelings first time. Say something to the person in the photo. It doesn't matter if it's a photo of one of your ancestors or one of yourself at any stage of your life.

'Dear So-and-so, you too are a part of the cosmic divine power and have boundless joy within you. In my

heart I see you laughing and in complete union with the elemental power. Peace and love be with you.' The more intensely you can feel this, and the more moved you are with happiness, the better. You'll never strengthen the old negative feelings about this person, or about this stage of your life, again. Remember the mirror neurones: we see someone whom we think of as tragic and send them exactly these vibrations. No surprise then if that person doesn't get any happier. The more intense your feelings are during this exercise, the purer and more constructive your thought-vibrations will be for this person or this stage of your life from now on.

At the same time, you'll be in a better mood yourself. When you see that formerly 'tragic' photo again, it will never again suck you into a swamp of negative feeling. Instead, the memory of the beautiful 'peace and love be with you' ritual will rise within you and you'll feel good and happy – about yourself and others.

The Turf Lawn Exercise for Learning How to Feel

This exercise also developed from the photo-album exercise. If you remember, we said earlier that you have to dig over the earth below before you lay new turf on top. In this exercise, old negative feelings are brought up and 'dug over'.

Everyone knows that if we let our shoulders droop and close our heart, every negative feeling gets even worse, so much so that they can feel as if they threaten our very existence. Pushing your shoulders back, breathing in deeply and opening your heart removes the threat from the feeling so that it can 'evaporate'.

For one month, set aside a particular time of day to 'practise feeling'. Observe yourself carefully during these periods and be watchful and deliberate in everything you do and feel. Observe your feelings! Consciously say the following to each feeling that comes your way, 'Hello, feeling. How are you? I'll let you be just you now, and I'm ready to accept you and feel you in all of your facets. I accept you completely.' By taking the role of the observer, you deny your ego the ability to identify with the feeling. Your divine cosmic elemental essence can rise to the surface and the feelings of your heart, the inner celebration of creation, will intensify.

This exercise helps you to distance yourself from feelings that appear automatically and from old blockages. In the light of conscious observation, these feelings are transformed.

Here are two examples of feelings that you might come across during this exercise. First off, guilt. If guilty feelings arise, simply think, 'OK, everything is my fault. So what?!' You'll see that, amazingly, this sentence evaporates the feeling of guilt! As guilt can only exist if you deny it. If you accept it, you also accept yourself. When you accept yourself, you can no longer feel guilty.

> Tip: wishing for feelings of happiness for everyone else increases your own feelings of happiness.

The other trick you can use is to be *thankful* for your faults. Just act as if the fault were a reason to be thankful, and give thanks for it intensely. It's fun, and it completely defuses the feeling. This makes the feeling evaporate. And on a deeper emotional level you strengthen the energy of thankfulness and happiness and so release your attachment to the fault.

As the Indian spiritual teacher Swami Kaleshwar once said, 'Only when you can love everything as it is can you change everything.'

You can use this technique to experiment with other feelings in the same way. Be open to whatever is created in this process, as the paths to healing and the inner images created will be different for each person.

Feelings carry their own solution within themselves. When negative or painful feelings are accepted completely, they dissipate.

You Don't Always Need to Know the Cause

... but it can shorten the path to freedom!

There is a myriad of individual thought patterns, as well as ones dictated by society, which we continue to cling to and which limit us. If we want to discover every single one before we overwrite it with something we wish for, we've an awful lot to do. This isn't always necessary, however. Many people who work with feelings use the principle that it's completely unnecessary always to know what the underlying causes are.

Energy follows attention, so why focus on things you don't want to have at all? It's much better to focus on the things you want to have.

In order to reformat the hard drive of your PC and save something new on it, all you need to know is how to reformat and which new things you want to save. You don't need to know what was on it before. This is how the unconscious functions as well.

> 'Formatting' works best when you're in a childlike and trusting state, with a lot of emotion, an open heart and the vision of your unconscious before you as a pure, white, blank page.
>
> To instil new habits you need energy and positive feelings to overcome the temptations within yourself (the old habits) until the new behaviour becomes a new pattern.

In our book *The Cosmic Ordering Service* we describe the technique of 'following a stronger responsibility towards yourself'. This makes us conscious of our smallest wishes and needs in the moment. Only through consciously creating and living in the present, completely without a thought for the past, do we begin to shed old patterns. The aim is to create positive feelings and to imagine and devote ourselves to the things that we want to achieve. In this way, instant cosmic ordering will have more power.

Remember that many paths lead to Rome. In this book, we have talked about re-examining old stored-up feelings. It is, however, very important that this re-examination doesn't become an addiction or an avoidance strategy. If you have been to ten, twenty, or more therapists over the years and have tried out hundreds of techniques, then it's probably time to start thinking about what you find so great about digging around in old things and why you don't want to get going and finally start living the new!

Overwriting Old Feelings

Overwriting old feelings once and for all means consciously paying attention to them in the here and now. With practice you learn to react to yourself and to what you're encountering honestly at any moment. The secret is that you begin to observe your feelings consciously: 'Oh, look at me. Now I'm beginning to feel inferior again, just because so-and-so said ...' A part of the feeling immediately starts to evaporate because you have recognized and observed it. It's as if that feeling of inferiority was locked up in your cell memory without even one ray of light falling on it, so it carried on growing blindly in the darkness of your subconscious, calling out from the depths for release.

> Suppressing unpleasant feelings keeps them locked up in the dark inside you. Examining them is the same as shining a light on them. Looking and feeling towards them is the same as opening the cell door inch by inch to free the imprisoned feeling. Then, what was threatening about the feeling, because it was unknown, evaporates.

If I panic in certain situations, and just lose my head and run away because I can't stand the feeling, it doesn't change anything. If on the other hand I examine it: 'What's actually going on inside me? How do I feel exactly at this moment? Where exactly in my body do I get this feeling?

How do I recognize this feeling?' then the process of release has already begun, and the pattern is broken. I have reminded myself of my true being and used this to observe a *pattern* in my unconscious. I have ended the identification with my ego and have returned to the perspective of my immortal spirit. There are no patterns saved here; the soul is free from all of these limitations.

> As soon as you unite yourself internally with this soul, this core of your being, you're as free again as the soul, in its natural way, always is.

There are limiting thought patterns that we've adopted from the society we live in, usually without even noticing it. PSYCK-K is a technique from the US which takes a long list of unfavourable thought patterns and filters out exactly those ones that weaken us and, by using a simple technique (connecting the two halves of the brain and anchoring the new), overwrites them with strong new thought patterns.

HNC (Human Neuro Cybrainetics www.cybrainetics.de) is another, more body-orientated method of treatment which uses the nervous system to test the effect of such patterns and to change them.

There are thought patterns that make your spiritual self, the core of your being, feel small or denied altogether, and force you to believe in a purely material world, which your spirit, of course, does not believe in. If you have adopted these thought patterns, they'll create a state of permanent conflict within you. The core of your being sees itself as a spiritual being which is experiencing the human. The world tries to make you think that it's the other way round, and that consciousness only exists given a specific mass of complex matter.

Only if you feel your way into the statements below precisely and observe your feelings to see if they apply to you, can you bring light into the darkness. It's possible that with some of them you will feel, 'How true! That explains why I put this or that irrational behaviour down to "having a bad day". Now I suddenly understand myself better …' Or you may feel that your heart is opening or that your soul is taking a deep breath, 'That's exactly it. Does that mean that I don't have to believe in …?'

By accepting the feeling, you're already setting it free. It might be true that the pattern has not always completely disappeared, but at least it's no longer growing in the dark, as you're now conscious of it.

Here are the statements for you to examine, to see if they limit the spiritual core of your being:

- I am frightened of being held captive by material things and the material world.
- I am frightened that, in the end, everything is built only on the material and I'll disappear when the material of my body disappears.
- I am frightened of being at the mercy of the material world.

- I am frightened that the divine power (the mind of the cosmos) isn't touching me or my life.
- I am deeply disappointed that the people on this planet aren't there to support each other. I thought that we were all one; how come I see only separation around me? Why can't I feel the oneness? Could it be that we're actually separate and not truly one?
- I am frightened of my own negative actions and thoughts.
- I am frightened of not being able to make it – not to be able to bring positive creations into my life.
- I am worried that perfect happiness on earth must be wrong. Don't you only get that in heaven after you have died? Won't I die sooner if I want to experience heaven now?

How did it go? Was there something there that sent a shiver down your spine, that really touched you? Bringing light into the darkness and experiencing the feeling consciously is the first step in this technique.

Uploading New Thought Processes

You can do this by concentrating on how it would feel if you already completely believed in a new principle, and had always believed in it and nothing else. What would your life be like then? Paint a picture in your mind and feel how it would be in your heart. Then, each time the old thought pattern comes to you again, don't push it away but invite it to come very close, like a friend. And then say this to the old thought pattern: 'I want to say something to you. I feel the need to transform you into … (and then describe your new principle). I wish that from now on you'll be … (and then name your new principle). Thank you for listening to me.'

Being addressed so lovingly will make the old thought pattern break down and transform itself for ever.

> Be loving to yourself and your old thought patterns.
> You aren't against the old, but for the new. You part
> from the old in love and invite the new in with love.

Here are some new principles – again, choose whichever appeal to you:

- I am certain that the material world only exists to make me happy.
- I am certain that the spiritual power of existence is the only thing that has ever worked within me.
- I am certain that the world is built on divine thoughts. So are my world, my body and so am I.
- I am certain that, deep down, everyone is here for one another after all, even when this isn't always visible on the surface.
- I am certain of the cosmic wisdom within me, which carries me and protects me.
- I am certain that I have already achieved all of the important things in life.

- I am certain that I'll only create complete and positive things.
- I am certain that all of my problems have already been solved positively and are now becoming visible, bit by bit.
- Paradise on earth is allowed.
- Paradise on earth is what we all need right now, to heal humankind and the natural world. It's not only allowed, it's what we need!

Old feelings and patterns can be overwritten if you consciously give them your attention. Those who strengthen the love and thankfulness within themselves don't always have to know which patterns they had before which prevented them from experiencing love.

Sometimes we get stuck and suddenly find that we can't move forward any more. Sometimes cosmic ordering works wonderfully for a while and then stops working suddenly. This can be a sign that we're being held back by an old pattern that's crying out for attention. By accepting our feelings and experiencing them fully, they begin to lose their power and make way for something new.

Thoughts Are There to Be Created!

We are now clear about the power of thoughts and the power of feelings, but I (Manfred) would still like to say something about the interplay between 'understanding' and 'feeling'. These are closely connected and can work together both in a positive and in a negative way. Since we've spoken so often about polarity and opposites, here is another way of looking at the connection from the point of view of the ego.

Our ego isn't that bad. When we work on our inner selves, we peel the layers from our ego and learn to experience our feelings as they really are, by accepting them into our hearts. Our ego can even help us do this. Separating our ego from our feelings helps us to examine our feelings with our hearts. This brings us into contact with our heart's desire and our ego even 'helps' by speaking to us, helping us to connect to ourselves.

Our ego is also invaluable in the area of our mind. Once we've learned to overcome the value judgements our ego carries out, we sort out the past and come to realize that the contradictions in our lives are only there to help us to find our ideals and wishes. Then our ego can help us to fulfil our wishes. We can look ahead and concentrate our thoughts and emotions on the now and on creating a wonderful future.

So thoughts aren't burdened by the ego when they are brought out into the light; our ego has become finer, our true self shines through and has taken control. The ego serves the heart, listens to our heart's desires, and becomes our spokesperson, telling them to the world. Feelings in the light are free of our ego, and can be recognized as being separate from it. Our ego no longer identifies itself with these feelings, but has cleared the way for the heart to experience the events of life. And, more importantly, the heart is listened to, it can express what it experiences. Brought full of light together into our life, feeling and rationality reach out to each other, working together to serve us and to be a powerful force for creation.

- Our rationality and our ego are there to help us decide what we want to create, and what we want to order from the cosmos.
- To pull the things we want into our lives, it isn't our *rationality* that we use. Our rationality cannot create a pull, only our feelings can!

> Don't be afraid of your ego. In its refined form it's a divine tool and full of beauty.

Experiencing – Heaven on Earth

What happens to those who begin to experience more and more, who find themselves and a connection to their inner core? What would a world be like where more and more people lived who were open to their emotional experience?

The Organs of Feeling Become Mature

True experience helps the organs of feeling to become mature. The feeling of being 'on top of the world' or 'in the depths of despair' which teenagers have is related to the development and growth of the organs of feeling. It's logical that someone with mature organs of feeling is less of a slave to their feelings. Someone who experiences isn't chained to their feelings. Instead, the feelings are sensed, accepted and released again. The feelings simply run through the person, leaving them free for the next experience. True being is therefore free of the extremes of feeling. The reason that the effects of feelings can be so great, even in later years, is above all that the ego isn't refined enough and is still too dominant: experi-

ences aren't accepted and feelings are judged very strongly. Some things are judged to be good, others bad. Life is then organized in such a way as to avoid bad feelings. Our lives are therefore not free, but directed by our fears and insecurities. However, avoidance is unsuccessful as unexperienced feelings seek to be repeated in order to be experienced. Nor does positive thinking help. Generally, great expressions of feeling show how adult and emotionally mature we really are as, completely independent of the age shown by our birth certificate, most of us are still children in spirit, on the way towards maturity.

Kindred Spirits Find Each Other

Something very beautiful happens as the spirit matures. Your own spiritual family begins to show itself. This has been our experience and that of many of our friends. A community of feeling is created, above and beyond the individual. You experience more as a group, and a wonderful openness to strangers is formed. You also notice that some people become closer than others; there's a spontaneous recognition and warmth of heart. This is your spiritual family: there will sometimes be a connection between two people experiencing their feelings, which might last a moment or even a whole lifetime.

Inner Beauty Shows Itself

Understanding and feeling with your heart is connected to the discovery that people are wonderfully beautiful inside. Regardless of what masks people wear, or which superficial games they play, inside they are wonderful and beautiful. The more you experience and accept, the more you understand the reasons for the behaviour of others, which then gives you a new perspective, making you more understanding and empathetic and teaching you to soften your ego. It's often the unobtrusive, shy people who have the most valuable treasures hidden within. They don't trust themselves to display them or share them, partly from a lack of knowledge of their own inner worth and also because the fine and pure aspects of a person only begin to show themselves when the self-important ego has learned to be quiet.

Beauty Is Recognized and Expressed

The Tipheret in the Kabbalah is the gateway to love, and is described using the words 'beauty' and 'empathy'. Coming into experience is connected to this, just as is the increasing connection to all people, animals and the natural world achieved through the organs of feeling. Even if the ego still enjoys judging, through experiencing we learn to be connected to everything, and then, like a gate, the beauty of nature and of people is opened to you. This is why the expression of goodness and beauty is a good indication for seeing how often your judgemental ego is quiet and the voice of your heart is free to express itself.

Be as the Little Children

By discovering the beauty of nature and the world, we approach the untroubled state a child is in when it runs about in the snow for the first time, finds a summer meadow, or watches a beetle. Be as a child again! This ancient quotation from the Bible means that we should forget all of our learning and growing up in order to return inside to the childlike state: innocent, naïve and non-judgemental.

You'll find your own way

My growth in experiencing has increasingly shown me my own way. How, after all, is my way supposed to show itself if I'm not connected to my spiritual core and my heart? I would only follow external signs and search, but not find. The path is connected to experiencing yourself, to hearing the voice that is speaking inside you and that wants to reveal itself. As I have already mentioned the Bible, here is one more tip on finding your own way. For a couple of years now, books and cassettes on the Aramaic form of the Lord's Prayer have been available written by Neil Douglas-Klotz. As it's believed that Jesus's mother tongue was Aramaic, Douglas-Klotz learned the language and studied the prayer in the original. He discovered that a single word might have a great number of meanings in Aramaic. So, for example, the word 'blood' also means wine, red and life. 'God' describes 'the divine mother', space, the cosmos, and oneness. The commonly used term 'sin' in Aramaic means 'to do something at the wrong moment' – harvesting grapes before they are ripe, for example. So the prayer hasn't got the fixed meaning that many of us have learned by heart. On the contrary, the original Aramaic invites us to create our own prayer. This is a divine invitation for us to find our own way, to trust 'the religion of our own heart' and to follow it more and more.

Discover Your Calling

The more we come to experience, the more we develop a particular meaning for our own lives: our 'blessing' reveals itself to us. Our blessing is something like a reason for our lives, or a talent. Just as for Barbel her calling is for writing, for others it might lie in healing, giving advice, or in craftsmanship. This calling can show itself in every area of life imaginable. You can tell because the energy flows more easily and things seem to come together automatically to form a whole. When we're 'blessed' we get strength and work seems to be effortless. It's as if the plug has been put in a socket. The blessed person somehow goes 'online' and taps into the energy and information they need without controlling it consciously.

Barbel has been known to sit at her desk and write with a cold for 20 hours at a go, and afterwards to feel well again! Writing connects her to the power of the source, and in this way is even able to heal her.

Become Love

How do we become our true selves? By shrugging off our old thought patterns, old beliefs that we've adopted from our parents, teachers and our surroundings. No one can truly know us; only we can grow more and more into our own true selves. 'Become what you have always been' is the blessing given by the Sufis since ancient times. They know that, for this to happen, parts of our consciousness, our thought patterns as well as our ego, have to be changed and transformed. 'There's no doubt that we'll become that which we believe we are.' But how can we achieve it? In some ways it's like the old conundrum of which came first, the chicken or the egg? How can I believe that I'm more than I think I am all by myself? Is there no one who can help me? Of course there are teachers, 'but the best teacher is the one who helps you to realize that you no longer need a teacher' (quotation from Dieter Hörner). A good teacher knows the yearning people have for external guidance, for giving up responsibility for their own lives, but as soon as you're able to define yourself using your own resources, you have made it. You are free of the opinions of others, you 'believe in yourself'. In future children will be able to change the world purely through this, that they carry the belief in themselves and the self-confidence within them from birth. It's a blessing and a very comforting thought, not only for parents, that someday children will be born in complete love and so will understand the world in a totally new way.

Love from Your Heart

In thinking about the children of this new age, we've already reached the future. What will the future be like if people increasingly live from the heart and through their experience? Is there a threshold which, when crossed, means that all people will be conscious of love and thankfulness? We will live to see it happen, that much is certain.

When I discover how to experience in the core of my being, there will be a whole range of wonderful 'side effects':

- The organs of sense reach maturity.
- You find your soul family.
- Your inner beauty shows itself.
- This beauty is recognized and expressed.
- We become more childlike once again.
- You find your own path.
- You discover the talent you are blessed with.
- You are more in love.
- You live more from the heart.

You and I – Two Perfect Mirrors

The most important stage of experience is naturally in the field of our relationships with others. Where else can we live out our joys and passions so fully? In addition to the concept already discussed – namely, that we attract certain events and pull them magically into our lives in order to truly experience them and then to internally release them – we would like to offer a further: that of the 'mirror'.

Our surroundings reflect our good or bad qualities back to us. You can find this idea in many spiritual and esoteric books. A well-known concept from psychoanalysis is the term 'projection': this means that we can only recognize certain qualities in others, but not in ourselves. This 'blind spot' in our self-awareness becomes ever smaller the more conscious we become of ourselves.

Waliha Cometti explains the law of the external mirror in this way:

Imagine that you particularly dislike a certain type of person, a certain colleague, neighbour or who-

ever. Now you enter a room with a thousand people in it. You don't know any of them, but sooner or later you'll find yourself sitting next to exactly the type of person that you can stand the least.

I (Barbel) often used to experience exactly how true this is. I remember, for example, a seminar I went to over 15 years ago with 50 participants, one of whom I found absolutely dreadful. He was exactly the type of person I would wish to be miles away from, and definitely not at a seminar in which I was also taking part. When the seminar began and everyone took a seat, this precise person promptly sat down next to me and started speaking to me at great length. Fantastic! The thing that shocked me most was when he told me that he knew hardly anyone at the seminar and had only sat down next to me because he had noticed me staring at him. He thought that this was a good sign. Gulp!

However, the seminar was actually really good and I transformed my repulsion towards this person without realizing it (that means the quality that I was above all rejecting within myself) and we even maintained a casual friendship for a few years afterwards. Had someone predicted this to me at the beginning of the seminar, I would have thought them completely mad.

This is what the law of the external mirror teaches us: if we're not in resonance with someone, we don't notice them. We tend to overlook them. As soon as we notice someone 'properly', there's a connection between us. Whether this is positive or negative doesn't actually matter. First impressions are reversible and transformable, as I so clearly experienced at that time.

Manfred's suggestion: trust yourself to take a look at exactly those people you have avoided up until now. What is it that bothers you most about them? Maybe there's something inside you that you can transform and which might even lead to a deep and enriching friendship? This doesn't mean that you have to listen to a whinger whining on at epic length, or that you should go out of your way to be dumped on. This will just pull you down too, and won't transform anyone.

I mean people who are quite friendly but whom you have chosen not to approach actively so far because they don't match your inner picture of a 'suitable' person to talk to.

Let's just go back to the example of the thousand people in the room and how, if we carry a strong feeling of rejection for some trait or type of person within us, we attract exactly that type of person. Waliha Cometti uses this example to demonstrate the power contained in our feelings. It's just that we usually don't notice this power at all.

We pull the things we reject into our lives, as if by magic. Because even the qualities that we don't want in our lives, or that we go so far as to reject, are still part of us! If we don't want to live them out or if we want to shut them out of our lives altogether, we create the environment around ourselves that will attract them into our lives.

The cosmos ensures that we become 'whole'. Either we become whole within ourselves or the cosmos supplies us with qualities we lack through our partners, our neighbours, colleagues or even chance acquaintances.

In astrology, for example, Mars has the attributes of aggressiveness and assertiveness. An unchecked Mars lives out his qualities and asserts himself. A checked Mars, in contrast, is hindered and his energy is repressed. With a Mars in check, his surroundings will take over the aggression for him and the 'wave trough' of aggression is compensated for by a 'wave crest' from his surroundings.

Once again, the saying of the mystics applies: 'As within, so without.' When what is inside you isn't lived out, or is rejected, it will be taken on by your surroundings and lived out 'on your behalf'. So what's there 'internally' but suppressed must be lived out in your external environment.

This is where the *wasifas* of the Sufis can be applied again. The quality that is missing in my life (e.g. aggression) can be activated using a particular *wasifa*. The fact that this quality is not obvious in us doesn't mean that it isn't there. On the contrary, the world surrounding us will automatically become less aggressive the more we allow our assertiveness to surface and accept it as part of us.

The ideal person is whole; 'You are what you are,' as the Sufis would say. A person who is whole lives out all of their qualities without suppressing anything inside or rejecting any part of themselves. Doing so also helps them to stop rejecting their surroundings, and they can begin to accept everything and every person just as they are.

Some people believe themselves to be whole, the finished article, by being only kind and nice. But if they haven't really examined the aggression within them, but have just suppressed it, they cause this aggression to express itself around them. Aggression is a state of feeling which, in energy terms, lies above depression and fear. It needs to be lived out and examined, experienced, so that you can truly come into your own power and into oneness with everything.

Like egotism, aggression is often misunderstood. Both have their positive sides. Being able to accept everything within and around us also means being able to love it. As with the example of aggression, thinking along these lines should cause you at some point to ask the question, 'Whose fault is it, then, if my neighbour, my partner, or the person sitting next to me on the train behaves aggressively towards me? What are my surroundings showing me?' The righteous, uptight ego will surely complain about these awful people, but the more refined ego will ask itself, 'What can I *learn* from this situation? What can I apply from it to my own life? Maybe this "awful" person is only acting in this way because I am creating it, because I need to be able to recognize myself in this mirror?'

I (Barbel) once had a colleague whom I wanted to be friendly to, but never managed it. She had a type of whinging submissiveness about her that always made my blood boil. I almost always responded to her in an unfriendly way, or not at all. Her manner drove me crazy. At the same time I also had a very aggressive client, to whom I was also far too submissive. Unluckily for me, I knew nothing about the laws of mirroring or attraction at that time, otherwise I would have realized that I could have used my overly submissive colleague as a mirror of the submissive parts of myself. If I had managed to get rid of these parts of myself, this colleague would probably not have had the power to annoy me any more. She, of course, could then have used *my* behaviour (and that of many others who felt the same as I did) to look inside herself. Instead, she just went on and on about how crap the world was and how mean everyone was to poor her.

The truth was that all around her were mirrors that could have showed her she was making herself unnaturally small. The company psychologist also told me once that this person's behaviour was a type of aggression, as she drove everyone around her to be aggressive by the way she acted, and then blamed them for it. The truth was that she was full of pent-up anger. Because she was very extreme in this, the reflections around her were also very extreme. Many colleagues reacted really nastily towards her, projecting bad feelings onto her without realizing what they were doing.

All of this shows us that the organ of feeling is made up of opposites. If I'm shy and sensitive, I should learn to be more assertive and more robust. As long as I reject parts of myself, my surroundings will always show me in what direction I still need to grow. Aggression is just an example. Any quality a person might have can be put in its stead: egotism, stubbornness, lack of consideration, abuse of power – and also altruism, conformity, consideration or powerlessness. We can find ourselves rejecting any human trait in others, but only because we reject it within ourselves.

When it comes down to it, the carousel of human feelings revolves around one point: self-love and self-acceptance. What does a person who acts aggressively towards me want to show me? 'You aren't good enough! You're worthless!' What does someone show me who leaves me, who rejects me, who pays me too little for my work, who passes me over for others, cheats me, puts me down, forces me to do things, sidelines me? The more I love myself, the more this will be reflected in the mirror of my surroundings. Whatever I put into my surroundings will also be given back to me. So self-love is certainly connected to a healthy kind of egotism, where the ego has learned that it can sometimes be aggressive and assertive in order to become whole. Only then, conscious of the overflow of love, can you share this bounty with others, happily and thankfully.

> If you approach others with a strong feeling such as anger or annoyance, you'll automatically attract other angry, annoyed people towards you.

This is why it's important, for example, to forgive ex-partners, otherwise you'll find that the next one is all too similar to the old.

This is the law of the mirror: the people who surround us reflect the way we are on the inside in their type and behaviour. Most of all, they reflect the level of self-love we've achieved so far!

The Animal Exercise

It's often not easy to dig down to the feelings stored in our unconsciousness, in order to release them. It can seem as if everything within us is fighting against this, and that some feelings are actually trying to hide themselves away. There's a trick, however, that can make it easy, where the part of us that fears change doesn't realize what is happening and doesn't activate its defence mechanisms. This fantastic trick is to imagine feelings as animals.

This is how the technique works:

- Think of the unwanted situation or the negative feeling as intensely as possible.
- If this feeling were an animal, what animal would it be? Imagine it however you like, from your own special creation through every possible mythical creature down to a simple worm or a glorious eagle.
- Your feeling is now an animal. How is this animal? How does it feel?

- What does the animal need to make it feel better? Everything is allowed here. Just think of a situation where conditions would be just right for the animal.

Let's take a look at this in practice with a sample session with Manfred and one of his clients who suffered from hay fever.

Manfred: 'How do you feel when you get hay fever?'

Client: 'Awful. I hate it.'

Manfred: 'Where in your body do you feel it? What exactly does it feel like?'

Client: 'I feel it throughout my entire body. Everything shimmers, just as the heat around us is shimmering now.'

Manfred: 'Try to feel it as precisely as possible. What other images come to mind?'

Client: 'It reminds me of summer holidays as a child. We were on the beach all day and, although it was much too hot and sandy and sticky for me, I couldn't get away and I had to stay there until my parents decided to leave. It always seemed to take for ever.'

Manfred: 'If the feeling of this memory were an animal, what animal would it be?'

Client: 'A huge fire-breathing dragon.'

Manfred: 'Please describe it even more exactly.'

Client: 'He has sticky skin with lots of sand stuck to it. Everything about him is hot and sticky.'

Manfred: 'How does the dragon feel?'

Client: 'Absolutely terrible. There's no way for him to escape the situation.'

Manfred: 'Ask the dragon with your thoughts, what he needs.'

Client (considering this tentatively, then, with an expression of wonder): 'Sympathy?'

Manfred: 'Why not? Open your heart and give him as much sympathy as you can. What's happening now?'

Client: 'He is feeling a bit better. The hopelessness of his situation doesn't seem quite as bad as before.'

Manfred: 'What's the worst thing about the situation he is in?'

Client: 'That he is trapped in it, that he can't change anything about it.'

Manfred: 'Are there any parallels to your hay fever?'

Client: 'Yes, I would say so, definitely. I think that the worst thing about it, really, is that I feel so trapped and totally exposed to it and I can't get away.'

Manfred: 'Then your very personal solution lies in fully accepting this feeling. Whenever you experience a hay fever attack, go right into that feeling of exposure. You have to immerse yourself in the feeling that you want to avoid in order to be able to release it. Always try to sense exactly which feeling you want to avoid, then feel it deliberately, as intensely as you can. But before your ego comes along and identifies itself with the feeling too closely, keep asking yourself where you feel it in your body and how precisely you can feel it. By observing the feeling, you remove the ability of your ego to attach itself to the feeling. Come on, let's try it. We'll walk through the flower garden outside and you can try to pinpoint and test the feeling.'

Outside, in the garden, the client promptly gets an attack of hay fever.

Client: 'I feel completely overwhelmed. There's nothing I can do. I don't have a chance ... Hello, feeling, I sense you, where exactly are you in my body? Oh, I can feel you, so that's where you are ... poor me, I'm the unhappiest person in the world. I have to put up with this curse and will never be able to do anything about it. I just have to bear it, poor me.'

Manfred: 'Where in your body do you sense this "unhappiest person in the world" feeling?'

Client (laughing): 'It's absurd. The feeling runs away when I try to find it. Somehow I have to laugh about myself, at how I'm standing here and trying to find the "unhappiest person in the world" feeling inside my body.'

They walk for a little while, with the client sniffing at all of the flowers to stimulate further attacks so that she can continue to observe the feeling. After a while she gives up. 'It's strange, normally I always try to avoid places that will trigger my hay fever, but today when I want to experience it to the full and to experience it as a feeling in every corner of my being, I have to invent tricks in order to cause an attack to happen. And the more I try to force it to happen, the more it disappears!'

Manfred: 'That must be really annoying ...'

The client looks surprised and then both she and Manfred burst out laughing.

Manfred: 'What feeling would you most like to associate with your hay fever?'

Client: 'To be free of my hay fever, fully free and untroubled.'

Manfred: 'Let's have another break and send this feeling out from the bottom of your heart to the whole of mankind. By wishing something for everyone, you increasingly pull it into your own life.'

> All feelings that you desperately want to avoid will do everything in their power to remain or reappear in your life.
>
> Using the image of an animal as a metaphor for the feeling and asking ourselves what the animal needs, helps us to find out what our feeling needs so that we can heal it.

BEING SINGLE

As another example, the more you try at all costs to avoid being single, the longer you'll stay single.

So look at the negative side: immerse yourself in the feeling that you want to avoid. Pinpoint the worst feeling you have when doing this. Where exactly is it in your body?

And the positive side: use the power of the negative feeling to make changes to yourself. Be creative, get to know yourself better and become the ideal partner that you would wish for yourself. Learn to love yourself. The more you say 'Yes' to this opportunity to work on yourself, the sooner your new partner will appear, and this time it will be someone with whom you can take the relationship to a higher, more harmonious level than has been possible so far.

BEING SHORT OF MONEY

Say you want to avoid being short of money at all costs. Be at one with your lack of money.

Look at the negative side: where exactly can you feel the poverty, this lack within your body? What feelings do you associate with being poor? For some it's a feeling of worthlessness, for others the lack of freedom to do what they want. It will be different for each of us, the feeling that we reject most. Be one with this feeling and observe it.

On the positive side: enjoy the simplicity (recommended reading: *Die Kunst des stilvollen Verarmens*

[*The Art of Becoming Poor with Style*], by Alexander von Schönburg), be creative, make a lot out of a little. And whenever you're given money, no matter how little, accept it with love and welcome it. Whenever you spend any money, be happy that you have something to spend. Be thankful for every penny that you're able to spend. If you feel positive every time you come into contact with money, you'll automatically be given more. If on the other hand you unconsciously keep 'evil money' away from you, the more negative feelings you will have about money whenever you are given any, spend any or even think about any. This is because your unconscious is trying to be kind to you, and protect you from things that make you feel bad.

HAVING PROBLEMS WITH YOUR PARTNER OR CHILDREN

I'm sure you've realized already that the more you reject something about your partner or your children, the more that thing occurs. Once again, take the feeling that you have in that particular situation, accept it fully and spend time and attention on self-love, regardless of what is happening around you. As soon as you have achieved this, the situation will change!

Important Note

Manfred's client in the animal exercise above was very lucky. She managed to improve her situation in just one session. Like everyone else, we like to take our great-

est success stories as an example, but we also want to be honest. You will often need more than just one session to achieve your particular goals. The reason why we often have to re-examine these deep-seated, long-suppressed feelings repeatedly lies in the difficulty we have in being completely honest with ourselves. We aren't used to doing this and our ego is a master at looking for escape routes. Just as we're approaching the core of our feeling and are on the path to releasing the attachment and identification of the ego to this feeling, our ego tells us that we urgently need to wash our hands, blow our nose, open the window or something else.

The ego knows that as soon as we've pinpointed the feeling and have brought it into the daylight of our conscious lives, then it's gone, and will turn into its opposite by itself! And this would be a calamity for the ego, as then it will have nothing more to complain about.

Therefore, allow yourself to be happy and promise your ego that you'll find it a new job and that you'll always love it, even if only to sing the praises of the whole world round the clock (which the refined ego does).

Exercises in Feeling for Instant Cosmic Ordering

As a cosmic orderer, I'm only interested in two things. If I absolutely desperately want to 'cancel' or change an order, what feeling do I want to avoid? Is there a feeling that it makes sense to integrate so that it can turn itself into its opposite?

And is this true of everything I order? Which feeling do I associate with the delivery? Where does the positive feeling of wishing perhaps already exist in my life? How can I strengthen it?

In *Cosmic Ordering: Complaints to the Universe*, we wrote about the techniques used by some Native American tribes. They consider what their life would be like if they already had the thing they were wishing for. What would their daily routine be like? How would they feel? What would be different? What would it feel like? They describe what it would be like in as much detail as possible. And when they have felt this as fully as possible, they give thanks, as if they have already received it. They believe that this pulls the wish into existence. The thing they warn against is repeatedly asking for the thing you want (repeated orders), as when we ask for something that we haven't got, we strengthen the feeling of lack, and create even more of a dearth. It's also important to the Native Americans to pay attention to the feeling you create around your wish. It must be positive and lively, in order to make the wish come true.

Only worries, doubts and fears can permanently cancel out positive orders. Examine the negative feelings: take the worries, doubts and fears and accept them fully. Feel them out to their very end. Be with them and observe where they reside in your body; stay with them as long as it takes until they evaporate, until you can be completely at peace with your current situation. Then there's nothing left to release. Then your instant cosmic order can zip off like an arrow towards its target.

Invite cosmic, divine consciousness to enter each one of the billions of cells in your body, open your heart and experience the cosmic oneness and elemental power within you. Ask for the reward in the problem, or how you can best divert the power of negative feeling and use it for your own advantage.

> Look around you and find the things that you love, just the way they are, no matter how small they are (your feel-good list). It could be your favourite pencil, the sun, a plant, your body etc.

Werner Ablass offers a great shortcut for the acceptance of negative feelings in his book *Leide nicht – liebe* (*Love, don't suffer*): love them, as they are. Love yourself even when you're angry, sad or annoyed. Love your anger, rejection and your feeling of annoyance – they are fantastic too, because if you love your anger, you no longer have to suppress it, but can feel it leisurely to its end. If you love your doubt, you no longer need to let it go, but can accept it fully, be with it and feel it to its end, until it turns itself into its opposite: into confidence!

> Pay attention to the feeling behind your instant cosmic order. Which feeling are you possibly trying to avoid, and which is the true feeling behind your wish?

Why Heartfelt Wishes Are Stronger

We've already heard quite a lot in this book about the impulses that drive the ego and its pleasure in the negative, so it's clear that pure 'ego wishes' often have a taste of 'wanting to avoid something' rather than 'wanting something for the pleasure of being'.

The energy of the heart, in contrast, is never an energy of complaint, but rather is connected to that part of us beyond our earthly selves, to the spiritual core of our being. The heart is connected to experience. Ideas and wishes that come from the heart can be childish, banal, funny, simply joyous or fulfilling; they can lead us to our calling or enrich the world. Whatever they may be, they are wishes that spring from our joy in something, or wishes that our soul wants to discover or experience, and therefore are wishes that have far more power than mere 'ego wishes'.

> If you pay attention to the positive feelings behind your wishes, then you are much nearer to the thing that your heart wants than to the thing that your reason has thought up superficially.

A classic example: my being wishes for freedom, but my reason thinks: a convertible, that's it. Open roof = freedom. But perhaps my heart is looking for a completely different kind of freedom – the freedom to make decisions for myself and not to let myself be dictated to by others. Maybe this is something that my reason, fearing for its very existence, hasn't even dared to think about.

Reason, ego, old thought patterns and fears work together, often without us even noticing it. We are far cleaner and purer in the essence of our wishes if we listen to our heart.

Talking of fear for one's existence, this is often an instinctive fear at the root of many other fears, such as the fear of 'failure' in important social situations. Something within us thinks secretly that our life is actually in danger. We often, for example, react in total panic when faced with a simple exam, or when we want to stand up for ourselves and our needs, as if our life were at stake. This has to do with the amygdala area of our brain, with ancient instincts that immediately turn on the 'flight' mechanism in our brains. This is explained very well in detail in the book *Erfolgsgefühle – Die emotionalen Grundlagen des Erfolges* (*Feelings of Success*) by Thomas Klüh.

> Ask yourself very consciously in each difficult situation whether your life is threatened by it, and see if the realization that this isn't the case calms you down in any way...

Back to our heart's desire: wishing for something for myself from the bottom of my heart means wishing for it with love, and love is the strongest force in the cosmos. Love contains – seen spiritually – the greatest amount of light. All matter consists of light, and light and love are the building materials from which everything is made. Therefore when I wish for something from my heart and out of love, this wish automatically contains more substance than a wish made without love. And therefore the wish is also more powerful.

In the next chapter another reason is given for why the heart's desires are stronger: the heart has the most direct connection to cosmic intelligence. This is not surprising. Everything consists of light and love, the heart generates light and love, so the qualities of the heart and everything that is made from it are the things that are closest to the elemental power.

> If you make a wish or order from the cosmos on the basis of a feeling of lack, or with a feeling of rejection, your wishes will have little power.

> Things that you order from the heart, you order out of love. Love is the strongest power in the cosmos. This means that the heart's desire is supported by the power of love.

The Feeling Prayer

Gregg Braden (author of the book *The Isaiah Effect*, which deals with the power of prayer) writes that 'the feeling prayer' can be found in very old religious texts, but that it then disappeared from later texts. When making a feeling prayer, the words and thoughts used serve to create the feeling within your heart that the thing you're praying for already exists. The original form of the feeling prayer, as described by Gregg Braden, is similar to the ancient technique used by the Native Americans: you imagine what it would be like if the thing you're wishing for were already there and, as soon as you can really feel it, you give thanks for it. By using the feeling prayer, you ensure that the process is managed by the power of the heart and that you feel as much love as possible while making it. A possible variant on this technique is that, after making the feeling prayer, you set yourself the task of doing as many little things as possible in your daily routine with your heart and so set up new and positive habits for yourself.

Barbel's tip: start off with a single, completely trivial activity that you do every day. For example, washing up, brushing your teeth, tidying, doing something with the children which you usually find stressful (such as getting them dressed – you'll know if you have children how difficult it can be to get them to the stage where they are all ready to go out), some annoying routine task at work, or anything else you choose. Choose one of these and decide from then on to do it with your heart, with enjoyment, and with thanks. Be thankful that you're able to carry out this task and enjoy it, as if it were the most fun you could have on earth. Maybe, when you were a child, you longed to be one of the 'big ones' who could brush their teeth by themselves, or something similar. Now you're big and can do it too, so go ahead and enjoy it.

Stick a note up about this task in a suitable place, so that you keep seeing it. Then really get into the habit of carrying out this task with love and joy. Let's take the example of brushing your teeth. Studies have shown that we clean our teeth more quickly, shower more quickly and eat more quickly than we did in the 1970s. And what do we do with the apparently extra 38 minutes of time we save? Watch TV. Great, what a great step forward. If you have chosen brushing your teeth, then decide to brush your teeth from now on as if it's a ritual you're carrying out, with the deepest inner pleasure. Brush your teeth meditatively. Brush them with thanks. Find joy in your bathroom, in your toothbrush with it's wonderfully rounded bristles. Love your teeth, tell them you value them through your thoughts, enjoy the feeling of the bristles against your gums, love the process of brushing your teeth and build yourself up to a teeth-brushing orgasm. Sorry, just a little joke.

I have tried this out, of course, and it was fascinating that after a while it was enough for me to see a picture of a toothbrush in an advert somewhere and I would start to relax and often automatically start grinning!

This technique can of course also be applied to making a cup of coffee, cleaning your shoes or the car, or opening your front door. Whenever you unlock something, do it with pleasure. Take a little moment to be thankful for the thing you're unlocking (the car, your home, your cupboard). Love the thing that you're unlocking and the act of unlocking it. Imagine that you're a little child who has just discovered how to use a key; use it with pleasure and joy.

All of this is a continuation of the feeling prayer, as you're giving a touch of conscious, positive feeling to small daily rituals. This will help you to raise, permanently, the basic way you feel, bit by bit, to raise your vibrations and the quality of the things that you're pulling into your life. And in increasing feelings of love, the rule is: *the more banal the reason, the purer the feeling!* We don't necessarily create a large amount of energy by doing great deeds, but we do by enjoying the love of creation in short moments of stillness and in childlike activities, free of any great objective. This is like an 'instant feeling prayer', a moment in which we let the concentrated vitality of life flow through us. The power of creation is produced in such moments because love and pure being grow out of them.

What nourishes the soul and your feelings:

- simplicity
- peace
- quiet
- deliberation
- yourself.

Redefining Working on Yourself: It's Right If It's Fun

There's a beautiful image in Korean Buddhism which comes from the Zen master Da Haeng Kun Sinim: 'When the inner doors to wisdom open, then you must be like a woodpecker: he drives his beak into the tree again and again, full of stamina and dedication, until his task is finished.'

Pecking a hole in a tree might sound like a long, hard slog to many people, but you have already made a start. While it might be quite a task if you were starting from near the bottom of the scale of feeling (deep melancholy) or if you hadn't started work on it. But the saying is '… be like a woodpecker', not 'be like a squirrel trying to create a woodpecker's nest' nor 'bang drearily away at the trunk, regardless of whether you're good at this or not'. The important thing is that the woodpecker has the greatest pleasure in building his nest. So don't think of working on yourself as being some strenuous or dull task. Discover the way to carry it out with happiness and great lightness.

Any feelings of strain or thoughts such as 'Oh no, now this is becoming such hard work' are logically counter-productive. They certainly won't allow your heart to begin to open.

Begin 'working on yourself' by opening your heart and finding more and more little and larger pleasures inside it. Begin by feeling your connection to the elemental power. You'll always be connected when you open your heart and keep a lookout for the finer feelings inside. It's fun. It's called spiritual work, but it's more like permanently giving yourself (spiritual) gifts – with great results.

As Einstein said: all nature aims towards harmony. What you're doing here by 'working' on your feelings and 'working' on yourself is uncovering your true nature, uncovering your joy, and having fun while doing it. The feeling of hard work is all old hat. Remember: the feeling creates the pull. So maybe you're sitting here and working away hard on yourself. What are you trying to achieve? The feeling you get is: 'This is difficult.' The result will be that it stays difficult. True work with your feelings comes from enjoying the process.

The high level of vibration that creates the pull from a feeling of joy comes when you experience the love of creation from your heart, from the confidence that you are doing well now and that you are living happily.

If I work hard on myself because everything about me is so wrong and I'm still so far away from everything being good and working well – what kind of vibration is that? What pull do I create from that? I make myself small and heavy, with a corresponding result. If you catch yourself doing this, then leave everything and meditate on the following sentences:

- I'm perfect the way I am. I love myself the way I am. The cosmos loves me, as I am. The only thing I have to do is to use the power of my own free will to decide which level of vibration I want to be at.
- Whether my vibrations are high or low – I'll always be OK the way I am, and the same amount of cosmic love will be available to me.
- Everything is good. I can open my heart at any time and let more cosmic love flow into me. I can also just leave it be. I will decide now, and love myself, no matter what choice I make.
- I'm allowed to be happy, but I don't have to be. If I want to pull happiness into my life, joy is the best feeling; it creates a pull for happy things. Do I want this? Yes? OK, then, I'll look around me now, here where I am at the moment, to see what I can find to concentrate on to make me feel at least a little bit happier, right here and at this moment in time. What can I think about that will make me feel good right now?

This is really the main part of the 'work'. It's like being a child and looking and feeling around you to see which game you want to play next.

And, by the way: however important it is to feel feelings through to their very end – if you wrap yourself up in doing this round the clock and have the feeling that there's still a huge amount buried inside you that still needs to be felt through to the very end and then released, it means you're travelling backwards again.

EXERCISE 1

Be happy now. Open your heart now. Discover the fine sense of feeling in your heart now. By doing this you sow the seeds for what you really want to grow in your life. Do it to raise your vibrations and to be truly present in this exact moment. This is the ideal state of mind to be in for receiving cosmic deliveries. In this state you're open to the little signals from within which let you do the right thing at the right time in order to make your wish come true.

EXERCISE 2

When a negative feeling appears in your day-to-day life, the trick is to take a deep breath, open your heart and to observe that feeling exactly! 'I can't manage that,' you say? But you manage to withdraw into yourself and to stick your head in the sand, which just makes everything even worse. From now on you're going to make it easier for yourself. Take a deep breath, open your heart and observe that feeling exactly! 'Who are you, feeling? Where are you in my body? What exactly do you feel like?' By identifying the feeling you draw out the worst of its venom, you prevent it from becoming an unconscious thought pattern and you give it the chance to turn itself into its opposite. Each feeling contains its opposite when it's felt to its fullest extent!

☆ Part III ☆

Practical Applications

Hotline to the Elemental Power

We have a TV in our guest bedroom, and sometimes I find Manfred in there glued to his horror films. One evening I discovered Manfred there, watching the final few minutes of a thriller. 'Stay here a moment, it's almost over,' he said, budging over on the sofa. In just these five minutes I saw about three zombies, a huge amount of blood and a blast of feelings of horror, fear and being trapped that I never would have come up with myself. And I was in an open, unguarded and, unfortunately, much too receptive mood.

My sister's husband also loves to watch this kind of stuff. I can't understand the evolutionary advantage that makes men enjoy it so much, but anyway, that night, surprise, surprise, I couldn't sleep. In my mind's eye I saw myself surrounded by a crowd of the undead, groaning because they couldn't find their way out of their inhospitable world. Gruesome. I began to worry that I would pull these creatures and their energy fields into my own energy field any second if I didn't stop thinking about them.

'Hello, cosmic elemental power, please come straight away,' I called out in my thoughts. 'I would like a direct connection to you, the source of all creation. I would like an immediate and direct connection to the part of the divine that contains nothing but light and love and the purity of being.'

While I was thinking this, the film *What Dreams May Come* with Robin Williams came to mind, as well as the books of Neale Donald Walsch, both of which repeatedly state, 'Hell isn't a place, but a state of mind. Neither is heaven a place, but a state of mind.' Similarly, the zombie domain isn't a place either, but a state of mind. How reassuring. I just have to direct my consciousness towards heaven and I'm already there. I firmly repeated: 'I refuse to accept anything but the pure divine power. Everyone else can create whatever they want and spend time in whatever state of mind they want to. At this precise moment, I am firmly fixing all of my attention and concentration on the divine elemental power, light and love. Nothing else interests me at this moment. Consciousness, where are you? I want to see pure love, pure light, the elemental power of creation, and nothing else.'

> The largest part of creation is made from pure love. You just have to be decisive and to concentrate enough and you will become aware of this elemental energy.

After I had breathed in a few times and had taken the divine elemental power and love deep into myself, the unhappy images evaporated altogether. Phew, what a relief. Yes, but wait a moment … then I started to wonder whether it wasn't a bit weak to climb back up into the lap of cosmic mum/dad/the elemental power in a panic and quiver with fear as soon as I was faced with something a little bit less than full of light. If everything is divine, then so are the more unpleasant creatures. They have just forgotten their divinity. Couldn't I do something to help them remember how much pleasanter it is to live in a heavenly rather than a hellish state of consciousness?

'Dear elemental power, as we're so well connected just now, couldn't you send me an idea of how I can connect heaven and hell for myself in a very non-judgemental and personal way, and in such a way that a person can choose freely between both and is also conscious of what they are choosing?'

As I concentrated my mind firmly on the energy of the elemental power, light and love, all of the negative feelings and fears evaporated and I was suddenly gripped by an overwhelmingly strong feeling of happiness and an urge to shout out loud with joy. It was in this mood of rejoicing that I had asked the question of the fear-free connection between heaven and hell. Of course, with me sending out such vibrations, the answer was there even before I had completely finished forming the question in my head. In my mind's eye I saw a new kind of amusement park before me: half was filled with things that are very close to our conscious idea of hell (terrifyingly steep rollercoasters loaded with zombies etc.) and the other half was filled with heavenly rides (a romantic ride with sweet scents and relaxing music etc.). Both halves were clearly separated from each other, and very different, but people were free to go to and fro between them. I dreamed my way through the park in minute detail and slept wonderfully, waking up after another dream in the morning. In this new dream, the zombies remembered how to reach the heavenly state of mind, after visiting my heaven-and-hell theme park, and suddenly found it very easy to cross over into heaven.

> 'Everything is made of the cosmic elemental power and so am I. I now choose the state of consciousness where I am fully connected to the elemental power with light and love.' You can use this exercise to meditate with, even if you're alone at midnight on top of the highest mountain.

Over time I developed a further exercise: I meditate or relax and say the following to myself: 'I imagine the divine elemental power to be in my heart. But I also know that it's in the heart of every single cell in my body. That makes billions of tiny units of divine consciousness inside my body. I concentrate on being aware of this divine spark in each of my cells. I am completely filled with this feeling. I know that the elemental power will work with my cells to give me optimum health.'

Both variations feel wonderful on all levels and give you the ideal basic feeling to create the pull needed for instant cosmic ordering. In cosmic ordering, exactly the same principle applies: the feeling of *separation* from the whole is what blocks us most from instant cosmic ordering. The stronger you feel separate from everything else, from nature and from the cosmic spirit, the more your internal 'fax machine' for ordering is jammed. 'No one's listening anyway' becomes your basic feeling, which then makes itself come true. You can only have thoughts like this when you feel separate from the elemental power within you.

So what is the feeling that supports every type of cosmic ordering? The feeling of *connection* and *unity* with the universal intelligence, the divine elemental power and with absolutely everything. If you are connected on a spiritual level with all other human beings, you can call on everyone else if you want to solve your problems in a positive way. Then others can meet you on this spiritual level and give you answers even without you having to say them out loud.

If you feel yourself connected to nature and the cosmic spirit, if you breathe the cosmic spirit in and breathe your being back into the cosmos with each breath, this living whole responds to your requests.

Heaven and hell aren't places, but states of consciousness. Feelings of separation or of being cut off from the source weaken you. Feelings of unity and connection with the whole, with the elemental power, strengthen you.

How to Use Negative Feelings

My 'zombie' experience made me think. It had started with feelings of fear and ended with a flight of creativity. Somehow, the power of fear had turned into the power of an idea. In the end I slept wonderfully. If I had just tried to suppress the feeling and to fall asleep in spite of it, I would have felt the next morning as if I had been on a drinking binge the night before. Suppressing negative feelings isn't good. They can be transformed.

So what else could I transform fear into? The next time I felt afraid, I tried to feel it as precisely as possible, to see what kind of power it really had. I found it to be destructive and very powerful. Hmm ... what could I do with a power like this? In the end, I imagined that the power of fear transformed itself into lots of little Pacmans which would race through me and use their incredible power of destruction on all the unhealthy things in my body. I imagined that I would be rejuvenated and strengthened through this process. I could do this for quite a long time before the fear-Pacmans finally ran out of power. I turned the exercise of feeling-to-the-end on the rest of the fear and then got out my feel-good list. When I was finished, I felt great again and strengthened by the whole process.

You can deal with rage, feelings of rejection, sadness and others in a very similar way. The more negative a feeling, the more power it has. Rage and aggression can be incredibly powerful. Why smash the furniture when you can put that energy to better use? While you have so much power available to you, think of what useful things you could do with it. Maybe this energy will allow you to do something that you would never manage to do normally? Is there something that you really want to do, but normally wouldn't dare? Maybe your moment of rage is a good time to write to your local MP and convince her to refurbish the local playground. As long as you're not angry with her, you won't even be tempted to be sarcastic or rude. But you can use the feeling of rage to overcome your usual reluctance to get involved. Nobody is really shy when they are angry.

> Use the power inside the feeling to do something positive.

One of the difficulties in writing this book is that there are so few standard solutions that apply to everything. Each feeling changes from moment to moment and requires a different solution. We keep using examples from our experience in the hope that they'll stimulate your creativity and joy in experimenting with your own feelings from moment to moment in an open way.

In times of mourning, loss and every kind of catastrophe, it's important not to suppress the feelings but to accept them as they are. *Becoming one with pain is the best remedy for it.* Then at some point it'll be over and won't become a long-term burden. At the same time, there's a hidden power and a gift in every sadness, which only you are able to find.

We hope that the previous two chapters have given you ideas of how to deal creatively with the power within negative feelings. Use the power. Then each negative feeling will turn into a gift in the end, but only you can discover it for yourself.

In the next chapter we'll look at the opposite – namely, how to use positive feelings to help with your instant cosmic ordering. Believe it or not, this is just as difficult to do as using negative ones!

The best remedy for pain is to become one with it.

Each negative feeling contains power. Use it!

Fear can make you creative, rage can release huge power. You can use your rage as a motor to finally get something specific done. Discover the power behind negative feelings, transform it and use it.

Every conflict, when you face up to it, contains an incredible gift.

The Great Advantage of Crimson Clouds of Feeling

Being positive – what we like to call 'crimson clouds of feeling' – are often ridiculed or even despised in our society. It is seen as uncool, childish and 'unrealistic'. We make a big fuss about all the negative things that happen and quickly chalk up the positive ones as naff. But as we've shown, from the point of view of the power of creation, this is completely the wrong way round. An Indian spiritual teacher (Swami Kaleshwar) who brings about the most amazing miracles says he's only able to do so because he has learned to find joy from the bottom of his heart in all existence. The biggest mistake we make in becoming whole is that we reject and avoid these wonderful feelings. What we should do, when we observe someone who is positive, is to rush over to them instead of running the other way feeling embarrassed. Even our sexuality has lost much of its depth of feeling through our general coolness. According to surveys, most women prefer romance, chocolate and bubble baths to sex. Sex is an important topic, as there's also a great deal of creative power in it. Nowadays more and more writers are writing about forms of sexuality that reactivate the depth of feeling and sensitivity/experience. *Making Love: Sexual Love the Divine Way* is a classic by Barry Long. *Peace between the Sheets* by Marnia Robinson is a more recent book from the US. Manfred and I share our experience of this type of sexuality in our book *Sex wie auf Wolke 7*. The aim is to return the divine energy and feeling to sexuality, so that it can unfold its inherent creative power again.

Do you remember the key question that lets you recognize the refined ego? When we act more and more from the heart and the ego becomes more refined, then we find joy in loving and praising the beautiful. We open our eyes and suddenly see the beauty around us, perhaps for the first time: the flowers, nature, people and things. We also give voice to this and begin to recognize and praise beauty more and more. We are increasingly thankful for our existence and the positive possibilities that our life offers us.

Positive feelings expand us, they let more energy through. Everybody can actually feel this as soon as they consciously compare the difference between positive and negative feelings. Feelings such as fear, doubt, coolness etc. cut us off from the flow of energy. Each of us can direct energy by cultivating the love inside us!

Each of us has the energy to heal within us; we just need to awaken it. This is done much better with positive feelings, love and thankfulness, than with coolness. Trying to be 'cool' and aloof kills our creative powers.

Being Allowed to and Having to

Because we have two five-year-old children (twins), we've been able to spend a lot of time on the subject of raising children (and no doubt will have to do more of this in future). A dear friend of ours once hit the nail on the head by saying that, however you try to raise your child is redundant in any case, as children always end up copying how their parents live.

As we were older when we became parents (around 40), we were lucky to get a very good au pair, and while the children were still very little we learned quite a lot from her. And, to come to the point, we compared her methods with the ones our parents used.

Some things become a lot clearer once you become a parent yourself. After having tried for a long time to do everything perfectly and to allow the children as much freedom as possible, we ended up at some point having to set boundaries.

Twins are a bit of a handful. We had our au pair, but no grandmas at hand, as they live too far away. Children need boundaries and firm rules; they more or less demand that adults say 'No'. But there has to be balance. Each 'No' should be followed by about three 'Yeses' (according to the spiritual teacher Waliha Cometti). Because if a child is refused too much too often, the 'not allowed' will become a cause of unhappiness and the child will grow up too much surrounded by this unhappy energy. The enthusiasm of the child will then be curbed and he will become shy and over-cautious. He might not dare to do some things any more at all, because he feels instinctively that he isn't allowed. It can also happen that such a child will become sulky: 'Fine, if you won't let me, then I don't even want to do it any more!' This is certainly no better.

Of course, parents only want the best for their children. Many think, 'Our child should have it easier than we did,' or something similar. And so we try to raise them and to direct them because we think we know what is right for them. Sometimes, however, our ambitions for our children overwhelm them. Sometimes we send the signal to our child: if you behave like this, I'll love you, but if you behave like that, I won't.

Our children are guided to a great extent only by feelings; it takes skill to sense what our children need and set them boundaries with sensitivity. Michelangelo said once that in hewing sculpture he simply had to remove the superfluous stone. We should bring up our children conscious of the fact that they arrive in the world with the highest potential, and we should be there only to support what is there already.

To help with this, why not create a 'sun of potential' for your child? Stick a good photo of your child in the middle of a plate-sized disc of coloured paper. Fix a lot of rays to the back of the disc, and on each one, you and the child's relations, friends, teachers etc. can write their thoughts on the child's potential. These can be qualities, skills, talents and/or personal strengths. Then you hang it up in the child's bedroom and, each time you look at it, ask yourself the question: 'Which of my child's qualities could I strengthen particularly today? How can I give my child the feeling of being wonderful, just as I know he is already?'

Our neighbour has a six-year-old child and worries about the fact that she already gets two hours of homework a week. The pressure on little children has been growing for several years now. What has happened to room for free development? What happens to the joy of learning when so much has to be learned for tests?

Barbel devotes a lot of time to this subject and therefore has lots of tips for parents on her children's book page and in her seminars. 'Fight it from the start' is her motto. If children are allowed to be happy, then the adults who care for them will be less frustrated. Children in our society have to do so many useless things and are allowed to do so little that nourishes their souls. That they can use their mobiles so much, watch lots of TV, and eat tons of sweets isn't really so valuable. If children have to do too much – or, to put it another way, are allowed to do too little – then the feelings that go with this will become fixed. Everyone says to them: 'You have to get good results to get a good job. You have to do an awful lot to earn a good salary. You have to work even when you're ill, otherwise you'll lose your job,' and so on. So many 'have tos'.

It can be very healing to spend a holiday somewhere where not everyone is tied up in the rat race. In the Brazilian countryside, for instance, people treat each other as people. *Everyone is respected and valued, just because they are human. Status is unimportant.* The pressure to perform, to 'have to', disappears completely. This can be a real eye-opener. Not that these kinds of societies don't also have their downside, but we could learn quite a healing lesson if we could try to learn something from their value systems.

You can sometimes also find this nearer to home. Here in Germany, those from the former East Germany had for many years little money, status or opportunity. The feeling of 'having to' is still not as widespread there as it is in the former West Germany. You are valued as a person there, even if you don't take part in the general 'having to'!

If our children grow up surrounded by the base vibration of 'having to', then 'being allowed to' remains miles away from us. The base vibration of 'have to' also means: I'm only allowed to do *this* once I have done *that*. We arrive in the world feeling 'allowed to' and are quickly taught the feeling of 'not allowed to'. The base energy of a child is joy and enthusiasm, but this turns very quickly into unhappiness in the face of too much 'having to'.

Let's look at this now in terms of feeling. Let's say that I have a stressful job and I 'have to' work 12 hours a day and even at the weekends. I 'have to' the whole day and am only 'allowed to' put my feet up on Sundays. What's the energy given out? Unhappiness, because I 'have to'. Can I expect that something I do unhappily will cause happiness for my boss, my colleagues or my clients? No, because this would contradict the law of resonance. I generally do my work feeling drained and in need of a holiday, and this will only bring me unhappiness back from my boss. But my boss is only returning to me what is already there anyway.

So what should I do? Above all it's about giving free rein to my 'allowed to' in order to give myself a better base vibration. Then it won't only be the instant cosmic ordering that works better; no, recognition at work will also not be long in coming.

In terms of relationships, you should also free your 'allowed to'. For example, you're allowed to go on holiday by yourself sometimes, you're allowed to meet up with friends, you're also allowed to take once in a while, rather than always giving.

'I'm allowed to' can also mean that you can say what you think to your partner, be angry, be different to how your partner would like you to be. Above all, you are allowed to listen to your joy: what does it want right now? This will then be reflected in all the areas of your life.

I'm allowed to have my own opinion. I can live completely differently to everyone else, eat what I want, drink what I want, spend my holidays how I want. Even if no one else understands, I'm allowed to.

Finally, just another word on the subject of anti-authoritarian child-rearing: if a child is allowed to do everything and doesn't know the meaning of 'not allowed to', the problem will only *seem* to be solved. Other, more serious problems will set in. This is why the anti-authoritarian methods of child-rearing have almost disappeared without trace. From the point of view of feeling, too little 'no' or 'not allowed to' can also affect their character and personality. A lack creates demand, as economists say, and this also applies to our inner self. If a child is allowed to do anything he wants, he'll find it very hard to orientate himself in the world. He won't develop yearnings, he won't have desires, but he won't be happy, either.

> Children need boundaries. If children are allowed to do too little, then this will become a fixture of their personality. The imprint will stay with them into adulthood. The 'having to do' replaces the childlike 'being allowed to do'. You have to get good results, work hard to earn a lot of money etc.
>
> If you always 'have to', then how do you feel? Unhappy!

New Firms in this New Age of Feeling

When people begin to pay more attention to themselves and their feelings, they won't just begin to make new and better decisions in their private lives, but in their work as well.

Here are two different scenarios. Let your mind dwell on them and pay attention to how you feel as you read them.

The Hastings family have just built a new house. Mr and Mrs Hastings earn good salaries and have got a large mortgage. The house is top-notch, but neither of them can afford to lose their jobs now. Neither of them can choose to change to working part-time just because they feel like it, otherwise they won't be able to meet the repayments. It's true that the house is fantastic, but the Hastings aren't really home much to enjoy it.

The Hoskins family have built a house. Mr and Mrs Hoskins earn good salaries and they haven't taken out a mortgage. The house is small, but cosy, and they are free of debt. They could both afford to lose their jobs. They could also both just work part-time if they wanted to, no problem, because they don't have to pay off a mortgage. It's true that the house isn't absolutely fantastic, but the Hoskins aren't at home that much because they are often on holiday.

So? How do you feel? I can tell you what *I* feel and you can compare. I'm sure you'll have felt different; everyone has their own impressions. The amazing house with the high mortgage on the border of we-can-just-about-afford-it gives me an impression of a superficial need to be taken seriously and the desire to keep up with the Joneses. At the same time this scenario makes me feel under a lot of pressure, and frustrated. I get the feeling that I wouldn't be allowed to rethink my life over the next 30 years. Everything will have to stay as it is; I'm a slave to the mortgage.

The little house without the mortgage gives me a feeling of lightness, freedom and real luxury. If I need luxury, I can book myself into the most expensive hotel in the world until I'm fed up with it, and I still won't need an overdraft to do it. I'm free to look into myself anew, to see where life is pulling me next. Everything is open and possible, because I have my independence.

Up until now we haven't questioned the system. We've thought, it has to be like this, we have to put expensive furniture into expensive offices and pay off high loans on them. Otherwise the clients won't come. We've ignored whether we feel put under pressure or not. After all, it's the norm. But maybe there's another way? What's so great about status anyway? Isn't quality of life far more important?

The more I can feel myself, the greater the desire I have to feel good. This feeling good includes feeling free, independent and also free of stress, pressure and the need for money.

Muhammad Yunus, the founder of the Grameen Bank for the poor in Bangladesh, and winner of the Nobel Peace Prize in 2006, had a repayment rate of 98 per cent in normal times and, in times of flood, still 89 per cent (I have written about this extraordinary man before; if you haven't read it, you can find the report free of charge in my online magazine at www.baerbelmohr.de). The industrial bank there has a repayment rate of 10 per cent. In 2000, Yunus already had an annual turnover of half a billion dollars a year. The secret of his success? He looked at what normal banks do, and did exactly the opposite!

More and more entrepreneurs are taking note. A new spirit is arising. These businesspeople simply want to feel good and to sleep soundly. This is more important than high recognition and all the rules of business. After a while you can't do anything else; the day comes when feeling good is more important than mere profit at any price.

A creative craftsman friend of ours told us this story:

At some point I didn't feel in the mood any more for clients who just create stress and then don't pay their bills for ages. Somehow I started to be able to recognize them more and more. Don't ask me how; they just seemed to radiate the fact. Why bother? I

*asked myself. You only live once and I can't spread
butter on a slice of bread more than once. I already
have everything I need. Now I just turn them down
straightaway. No time, I'm very sorry, I'm fully
booked. Well, then something strange happened.
After a while they just stayed away by themselves,
and other clients started coming. It was as if it had
been passed round in a kind of spiritual network,
that I'm one of those people who doesn't just work
for money, but that it should also be enjoyable. At
some point I also began to have more money left
over than before. I don't understand exactly what
happened, but it's definitely a good thing.*

So much for a statement from a Bavarian backwater. I have
had similar reports from Berlin, Frankfurt and Zurich. It's
not enough for these new businesspeople to work just for
money, and they're increasing in number. And they prefer
to do business with those who think the same way.

Whoever is more in touch with their feelings changes
their aspirations. Suddenly they want to feel good at
work and this becomes more important, bit by bit,
than profit or status.

Then something amazing happens: instead of profits
sinking, they actually rise. Because there are more and
more people who value feeling good at work and who
want to work with others who feel the same way!

The Last Shall Come First

Maybe you want to have a great career and make it right to the top. That's just the way you are. Or you feel that it's not about having a career, you're just fed up with always coming last. Or, perhaps, somewhere inside, you do want to feel very big and to be first. Is there a trick that will help you to achieve this? Yes! And here it is: the last shall come first.

Above all, if you want to be something, you have to experience the opposite. You can't have a feeling for 'quiet' perfection when you haven't experienced the 'loud' kind. Your value judgement of feeling a connection with others is intensified if you've spent long periods alone in your life. You can value the peace of the countryside twice as much if you've lived in a loud city for a long time. Whichever way round, each feeling is more intense if you have experienced its opposite.

In the same way, it's easier for you to be first if you have known the feeling of being last and can accept yourself the way you are, in spite of all. If you haven't first experienced being last, then your stay at the top will be short-lived. Why? Imagine a person with a feeling of low self-esteem who reacts with panic to rejection and the feeling of not being able to keep up. This person then becomes a popstar. I (Barbel) worked in the music industry as a photographic assistant when I was young, and learned quite a lot about this experience. A new star of course goes crazy with enthusiasm. She is finally getting all the attention and plaudits that she has always wished for. But she is also panicking: 'This must never end, whatever happens, I can't fall as low as I was before.' Now, all of us know how long most pop stars last – namely, not long. A career might be good for a maximum of five years, then there's no call for our flash-in-the-pan any more. And more than one has committed suicide afterwards. This kind of person constantly makes bad decisions as a result of their fear of falling, as intuition no longer works under the influence of fear. This kind of person might also accept bad or unfair, just to prevent her fame slipping away from her. Of course, there are all kinds of people in show business. There are stars who don't let themselves be manipulated. Either things happen the way they think are right, or they don't happen at all. Unmoved, these people just shrug when they are offered bad contracts or other deals and say, 'Well then, it's not meant to be.'

The difference is clear. One can make herself feel at home, even way down on the bottom rung of society's status ladder, and the other can't.

> The more you can go into the feeling of being last, the more you can experience it fully until you arrive back at the feeling of joy, the more secure you'll be on the mountain peak.

I wonder if you're familiar with the saying: 'Once your reputation has been ruined, life is free and easy'? Experiencing failure to its end forms a new basis for power and experience.

It's very similar for people who spend years on the edge of ruin, in a panic fighting to save their business from bankruptcy. Then, when it finally happens and it's all over, they actually feel rather relieved.

In some companies, formerly bankrupt people are often gladly taken as CEOs. Why? Because they have had the experience. They know the feeling of being right at the bottom and this gives them a feeling of peace and calm. This peace and calm gives them valuable stability and good intuition the next time round. This time they have their priorities in order; they know what is important.

Of course, there are also people who never learn from their experience. But take a closer look: maybe they have never truly accepted failure and are still fighting it, so all the while are still suppressing their own mistakes. Then only one thing can happen: they will make the same mistake again and again. The only ones who are strong are those who have worked through their feeling completely.

If you want to be first at something, then don't run away from the experience of being last. Act towards the feeling as with the turf exercise: deep breath, open heart and become one with the feeling and speak with it from the point of view of an observer: 'Hello, feeling, who are you? Show yourself. You are allowed to exist, I accept you.' Even in being last, the clouds of fear will eventually part and you'll see the blue sky. And the sky here is peaceful calm and self-love, even if at the moment you're last.

Just imagine that you start climbing up the mountain with this feeling and finally get to the peak. No matter what peak it is. And imagine then that some crook comes along. With your background of peaceful calm and self-love, and a secure place on the ground at the bottom, you are untouchable. You know that you can go back to the bottom at any time and that being there is also good. And because you know that it's also good there, and that there's nothing to fear, then you can just as easily stay at the top and watch calmly as all of those clinging to the peak in panic drop off one by one.

We have a guest trainer in our life-enjoyment seminars, Dieter M. Hörner. He has been a trainer for over 20 years and holds a two-hour course in our seminars. While he was still very young, there was a time when he made a turnover of 100 million Swiss Francs. This happened very quickly and unexpectedly. He hadn't had the feeling of being last by then. He started panicking about whether he could manage it all, started making one wrong decision after another and was soon completely bankrupt.

He was right back at the bottom. What did he do? He got up and started marching back up the mountain. Everyone who hears him speak senses the power of his experience and it's fantastic how much they trust him. They sense his power and calm poise, and trust themselves more straight-away once they have experienced him.

Maybe you don't want to have a career, but be more like a human version of a polished diamond. Even then you need to have experienced the feeling of being the opposite. Manfred signed up to a course entitled 'Nothing Embarrasses Me' for this very reason. This is what he says:

> *Because being 'last' is difficult for me, but I see the value of it, I made a deal with myself: the 'I'm not embarrassed by anything' agreement. To be honest, this wasn't initially my idea, but was suggested by a dear friend, Eyk. The course is very easy and goes like this: whenever you're faced in life with the choice of doing something, or even having to do something that looks like it'll be uncomfortable, say to yourself: 'Nothing embarrasses me!' Then just go ahead and do it. After a while this becomes a habit. This could be public speaking, performing on stage, wearing crazy clothes, whatever. I vividly remember my appearance in the ashram in Sri Bala Sai Baba when the guru asked to be entertained and everyone looked away in embarrassment. As I was bound by my agreement, I looked about me with a friendly*

smile, and was invited to perform a snake dance
with two Indian women, unrehearsed, of course,
(and of course with a soft-toy snake). Since then
I'm known as 'Mr Snake' in the chronicles of the
ashram, and the guru was very amused.
According to my 'Nothing embarrasses me' course,
I have repeatedly confronted myself with being
'last', the stupidest, the person who can be convinced to try any daft idea. Everyone else was
allowed to laugh at me as much as they wanted.
In this self-experiment I have repeatedly felt put-
down, laughed at and judged as coming last. I'm
also subject to the judgement of my own ego, which
is watching, and which naturally finds it unbearable. Shame and disgrace are the chief feelings. But
each time this happens I find a completely different
power growing up from beneath them, as the more
I can cut my ego down to size, the more I dare to do
the opposite. The organ of sense is also an organ of
opposites, and the more I can bring my shame into
existence, the more my success will manifest itself.
You don't believe me? Try it! It's an open course
and everyone is allowed to have a go. If you're a
man, it doesn't have to mean dressing up in a little
black dress and dancing on a table in front of 50
guests like our friend Paulus recently. Hats off to
Paulus!

The last will come first

- because they have nothing to fear
- because they are more stable
- because they value the feeling of being first more greatly
- because they are calmer
- because they can rely on their intuition without fear!

Feeling Your Way to Greater Physical Health

Did you know that we no longer say 'Gesundheit' (health) when someone sneezes? It's totally out because it automatically gives rise to the feeling that health is what the person is lacking at that moment. If someone sneezes often and keeps hearing 'Gesundheit, Gesundheit – come on, stop being poorly,' it may be polite, but it's not a good message to be giving his unconscious. We now say 'Stay healthy!' because it feels better. *Achoo* – and straight away comes 'Stay healthy!'

Health has a lot to do with our basic feelings in life. Gentle therapies that help us to rediscover the beauty within us, instead of wallowing in old complexes the whole time, make increasing sense nowadays. By no means does this mean that we should shut out our dark sides, but precisely the opposite: we should recognize them and incorporate them into ourselves again with love.

Because I'm human, I naturally have dark sides to me, and it makes sense to recognize them because otherwise they gain attention for themselves through uncontrolled breakouts. This is exactly the same for suppressed feelings. The more I know all the facets of myself, the freer I am in choosing who I want to be. Only when I know that I have stupidity within me can I give preference to my wisdom. To do this, however, I surely don't need to feel guilty about these dark sides and neither do I need any accusing fingers pointed at me and no sledgehammer methods to accept them. Being nice to yourself isn't only allowed, it's a sensible method of healing!

By the way, this reminds me of a book by Thomas Klüh (*Mein Weg zum Glück* [*My Way to Happiness*], www.thomasklueh.de), which I have just read. Thomas describes how people have three happiness centres in their brains: a centre for feelings of attachment, one for enjoyment, and one for appetite (the appetite for something, the appetite to do something). This explains why our seminar (mine and Thomas's), which actually is for strengthening the intuition, becoming consciously realistic and being happier more often, also seems additionally to stabilize health. I have had this feedback from participants. The more they find attachment, enjoyment, happiness and an appetite for life, the healthier they become.

> Becoming and remaining healthy is about the process of self-experience and the realization of basic human needs: attachment, closeness, the joy of being etc. Above all, it's about our connection to the cosmic elemental power within us.

A healer is therefore better the more they can encourage their clients to reconnect themselves to the elemental power, as this is actually what the body and spirit are searching for. Here is a story from one of my friends, the manager of a mid-sized company:

I often work 60 hours a week, or even more. Sometimes I just can't face it any more, but I have to do it. We can't budget for more employees at the moment and when I have made appointments with clients, then I also want to honour them. I just have to get stuck in. Sometimes I get the feeling that I'm just about to collapse. Then I do something that I have learned to do really well by now: I sit myself down quietly for a few moments and speak directly with the cells in my body in a friendly way. I know that there are several billion of them, and I imagine that all of these billions are listening to me.

'Dear cells, I know that you need energy in order to regenerate yourselves. I also know, though, that sleep is only one way to get energy. I know that you're all part of divine creation and that in truth all energy flows from this anyway. Please open yourselves up now to the cosmic power and re-energize yourselves. Please could you recharge yourselves as if you had had ten hours' sleep and a three-hour walk in the countryside and a meal after that? In return, I promise you that I really

will make up for it at the weekend with sleep, walks in the countryside and freshly pressed fruit juice. Please just support me over the next three days (or however many it is).'

Sometimes I have to carry on doing this for five minutes, but then I'm top-fit again and ready for action. But, having said this, I also have these damned digestion problems and pain in my knees. A few weeks ago I asked myself if I was an idiot after all. I find it completely normal to be fit again after five minutes as if I had slept for ten hours, because it works. Why don't I just generate the energy that I need to control my digestion and to repair my knee, whatever the problem is there?

This gentleman tried it and swears that since then his knee and his digestion have both got better. His secret? You have to be able to feel it! You have to treat the cells as if they were individuals and take them seriously and value them. You have to be aware of the fact that they are making an extraordinary effort on your behalf and value and thank them appropriately! And then there have to be times when you do everything that your body wishes you to do. Then the cells will be right behind you when you need their full effort.

A book has been published called *The Wisdom of Your Cells* by the microbiologist Bruce Lipton. He comes to the same conclusion, that every cell in the body has its own intelligence and that you can communicate with your own cells. According to Lipton, people are a kind of alliance of many individual little units of consciousness. When you give the order, 'All cells go online now and connect to the cosmic elemental power. Elemental power, please recharge them and restore their natural harmony,' (according to Einstein, everything naturally tends towards harmony, if we would only allow it), then each individual cell actually connects to the cosmos and optimizes its level of energy and health.

This works when it's only a thought concept, but when you send the message to your cells in the form of a positive feeling, then you have a real turbo-booster behind it. How far can this take you? Read the example of Walter Russell in the next chapter. What we believe in will become our reality. It's up to us to build up our belief bit by bit.

The closer we feel connected to the elemental power, the healthier we are.

Love Is the Strongest Power in the Cosmos

Is love really stronger than hate and fear, or could it be that when we are feeling hate or anger, we simply can't hold the channel open for energy and love? Let's take a very small example and a very big example to have a look at what can happen when we bring more of the love energy into our lives.

I had made some strawberry ice cream for my children. I used stevia instead of sugar, and organic strawberries. The children shared it with a child from next door while I was mowing the lawn. Hannah, the little girl from next door (aged five, just as our twins are) found that the ice cream was too hard and, because she is a very forward little lady, she decided to tell me off for it. She told my twins what she was going to do and strode off into the garden to tell me off. My little ones were appalled. 'She can't tell our mum off!' And they ran after her in a fluster. From a long way off (well, not so very far – our garden isn't that large!) the twins called out, 'Mama, we love you!' They wanted to console me in advance, so I wouldn't be sad about the telling off I was about to get. Their little friend, who had been marching towards me, became disconcerted and stopped. I could see that the wind had been completely taken out of her sails by what my children were calling out to me (though I didn't know what it was all about). She stood there for a moment in uncertainty, then turned around and ran off home to her mother. My two then told me what had happened.

A week later they were clearly still trying to come to terms with this little episode, as one of them asked me one evening before falling asleep, 'Mama, why did Hannah run off like that when we told you that we loved you?' 'Because you radiated so much love. Telling me off then didn't fit in with her plan, and that's what she realized,' I tried to explain.

If love is truly clear and pure, and can reach the other person, then all aggressive intentions evaporate by themselves. The problem is, how can we communicate love so that it really does reach the other person?

Our big example should help with this. It's taken from the artist, philosopher and natural scientist, Walter Russell (1871–1963):

When I was fourteen I became sick with black diphtheria, a disease that is identical to the Black Death. Samples from my throat made the blade of a penknife so black that the doctors said I would never survive, as the function of my throat had been completely destroyed.

*A little later the doctors declared I was dead. The
undertakers had already arrived. I had no consciousness of my body, none whatsoever, but in this
state a huge feeling of ecstasy came over me, filling
me with the all-knowing light of love and then I got
up from my bed, much to the surprise of my griev-
ing parents, completely cured. A new examination
of my throat showed it to be completely normal
healthy tissue and my weakened body was strong
and vital again.*

*This clearly shows, together with the principles list-
ed already, the fact that the complete balance that
a human being can only reach in the full awareness
of the unity of God and mankind, can make each
person who has been enlightened in this way, the
master of the electrical waves from which his body
is constructed.'*

(Taken from Die Botschaft der Göttlichen Iliade
[The Message of the Divine Iliad], *page 273, with
permission from Genius Publishing,
www.genius-verlag.de)*

Joseph McMoneagle, the successful psychic who worked
for the American counter-intelligence services for decades
and located objects and also people who had been kid-
napped or had disappeared in other ways using the power
of his mind, gained his powers suddenly after a near-death
experience. A friend of mine and my husband unexpect-

edly gained strong spiritual healing powers in a situation in which she also nearly died. A great many healers whom I have got to know in the course of my life gained their powers or greatly increased them at a time in which they themselves were seriously ill.

I think that we can find a confirmation in this phenomenon of the theory of opposites, which states that we must experience a thing's opposite in order to become whole or to experience fully. In order to experience pure love and its unbounded power of healing, it may be true that we have to experience the opposite, namely death.

'How gruesome,' you might be thinking. 'I would dearly love to develop my own powers of healing and pure love within me, but can't I somehow spare myself the near-death experience?' Yes, I think you can. By fully experiencing the feeling of being cut off from everything, and this with an open heart. What's the maximum amount of isolation that you can personally imagine in your life? If you can fully experience this feeling of total separation on all levels, you'll arrive at the same place where Walter Russell found his incredible healing and transformative energy: in great ecstasy with the all-knowing light of love!

It's a little like Yin and Yang. If, for example, you enter the full energy of Yin, at its zenith it'll turn into Yang. Therefore you never have to ask yourself whether you're completely crazy because you keep heaping up so many problems in life. Maybe you just do this in order to experience the absolute flash afterwards, in which you re-enter the oneness.

This is a bit like someone who, because of a food allergy, has to live for two months on plain rice and nothing else. If such a person is then allowed to taste a drop of tomato sauce, then the taste experience they get is probably one of the most memorable and happiest of their lives.

You probably also sometimes go on a 'happiness diet' (a diet that excludes happiness) in order to savour it later through expanded senses and a more finely-tuned sense of awareness. So there's no point in blaming yourself for it. You can simply decide to end your withdrawal from happiness or luck or the feeling of separation again now. Take your first taste of cosmic tomato sauce by focusing your attention, little by little, on more happy feelings.

This could be the end of the chapter. But I don't want to finish until I have mentioned that you can combat all of the challenges and problems that turn up on a daily basis by opening your heart and giving them all the love you can. This may seem absurd at first, but it takes all of these problems to a completely new level and converts them into positive and harmless entities. 'Dear problem, since you're here now, I don't want to miss the opportunity of welcoming you from the bottom of my heart. I accept the gift that lies within you with deep thankfulness.'

You can't begin to imagine the creative potential and the unending power that flow into you when you approach problems in this manner, with an open heart. You have to have tried it to understand. Then anything can happen, from the very small to the very largest of miracles.

'Dear problem, I thank you!'

Love is the greatest power in the cosmos. If you can experience a feeling such as isolation with an open heart, you might suddenly find yourself in a feeling of complete happiness again.

You can also open your heart to all of the problems that turn up in your daily life and give them all of your love. 'Dear problem, since you're here now, I don't want to miss the opportunity of welcoming you from the bottom of my heart. I accept the gift that lies within you with deep thankfulness.'

Wishing for World Peace

If repeating thoughts and feelings make them become reality, what reality do we create if we begin the day by
reading the latest news about war, terror and catastrophe
round the world? And end the day by watching the same
things again on TV?

> Energy follows attention.

What energy do you want to send the world? Begin and
end your day with positive thoughts about the world. You
can remove the free will of others in this way and somehow force them, through the power of your thoughts, to
live the way you think is right. But you can also change
your own personal world and take on responsibility for
what you contribute to the world in terms of thought fields
and the quality of feeling. Remember: everything is connected. Your thoughts about the world might be a drop in
the ocean. But wouldn't you rather be a pure, clear drop

that propagates beauty than one that just adds more dirt to everything?

Focus your attention on the large and small beauties of this world and send the world your love and thanks for them. Indulge yourself in your positive feelings of joy and beauty for the world. In this way you'll sow better seeds than if you worry constantly about the world from morning to night. In this small way you change the things that you encounter in the world in a positive way and you'll generally infect others with your positivity, and we'll all reap a world with common streams of thought allowing the creation of new solutions, new paths, ideas and a new consciousness.

So What About World Peace?

Do we want world peace because we fear war or because we would prefer to live in peace? If it's the first, and the fear of war lurks inside us, fear is the feeling we send out into the world, and this gives war greater energy. If I personally want to live in peace, then I should order/wish for/visualize it in this way: 'I like living in peace, I enjoy peace wherever I find it.' In this way I turn my attention to peace and therefore to the thing I want to create.

What else can be changed in this way? The New Zealand healer Clif Sanderson told me about an island which he had visited and that is so flat that when typhoons come it's regularly completely flooded for months. Even so, people live there and the island has been inhabited for thousands of years. 'How do you cope?' Clif asked them, and they answered that they observe nature. They can tell from the plants if a typhoon is headed their way any time in the next six months. Then they pack up their things and look for an island which doesn't show these signs, and then they move there and wait until the typhoon has passed over. This seems to work, otherwise these tribes would have died out long ago. (Clif has described this occurrence in his book *Knowing Nothing, Living Happy*. You can also order his book through www.intention-in-action.com.)

It's exactly the same when I focus my attention on the energy of peace. I won't always be able to secure peace in my town, but life will begin to send me signs of when it's time to move on, so that I can continue to live my life in peace.

The Hawaiian Art of Peace Meditation

Ho'oponopono is a Hawaiian healing technique. It's composed of various elements, one of which is to heal everything in the world that makes you feel unwell.

The ancient Hawaiians believed that we are fully responsible for everything that happens. In modern-day terms this would include terrorist attacks, politics and the state of the economy as much as the behaviour of our close relatives and acquaintances. This way of looking at life asserts that none of these things actually exists except as a projection of our inner selves. *The problem, therefore, isn't that of others, but our own.* Because the whole world is our own creation! Everything that happens in my world is created by me, otherwise it would not happen in my world. But we're not powerless, as everything that we notice and do not like wants to be healed by us.

How on earth are we supposed to do this? According to *Ho'oponopono*, this is incredibly easy. Let's take an example. Someone has a problem and we want to heal them or help the problem to be solved in a positive way. We imagine what it would be like if we had this problem. What problem inside ourselves could have caused their problem? When we get an image or a feeling of how we might have caused the problem, then we heal this part of the problem inside ourselves with the simple words, 'I'm sorry' and 'I love you.' This sounds far too simple to have any kind of effect, but you have a try and see how powerful it can be.

If you try to send an aggressive colleague light and love, they might become raging mad because they don't want to have your energy. But with *Ho'oponopono*, you don't send them anything. You only consider: 'If I were this person – why would I act like that?' And then you heal that part with 'I'm sorry' and 'I love you.' Try it out. Even if the other person doesn't change, it'll change your attitude towards them. Instead of the anger or fear you felt for them, instead of the stress and tension you feel just by seeing them walking down the corridor, you'll suddenly feel sympathy and understanding, because you'll understand why they might act the way they do. You have released the resonance within you towards this problem and you'll see that it no longer affects you. Whatever they do, you stay relaxed. Just this is worth its weight in gold. But if it works really well, then they'll even change themselves. Sometimes only in relation to you, but sometimes completely.

I once got a report of this technique by email and forwarded it to my circle of friends, which triggered a wave of experimentation. The biggest successes were immediate peace (within a single day) between a divorced couple, who normally wound each other up terribly. Full of enthusiasm, another friend tried it out next day with her mother-in-law (whom she had real stress with). The feeling of stress gave way immediately to understanding sympathy. The mother-in-law also noticed that the vibrations had changed and also reacted in a more friendly way.

I must say here, however – and I find this important – that you'll by no means always discover the true reasons motivating the other person. You'll only find your resonance towards their kind of behaviour. Whereas before you might have thought, 'Only a crazy person would act like this; it's totally irrational,' you'll find yourself thinking, 'Yes, I can imagine that you might not know any better, if you really felt that way.' *It's a huge relief if you're not forced to view the other person negatively any more, but rather can look at them with empathy!*

As Waliha Cometti says: 'If I do act as if something isn't inside me, I strengthen it externally. This technique shows me the truth, and only in this way can I release it.'

Test out the *Ho'oponopono* technique for yourself. Let's imagine again my former co-worker who was really submissive. Imagine yourself approaching others in this way, with your head hung low and a quiet and totally sub-servient voice. Why would you be like this? What would be happening inside you? For myself, I might do it because I wanted to act the 'poor victim' and behind each of my words would lie the accusation, 'You're all sooo horrible, while I'm the only one who's really nice.'

Looking within yourself, maybe you'll find completely different motivating factors. Whatever you find, say to it, 'I'm sorry' and 'I love you.' You aren't saying this to the submissive colleague or the submissive fantasy person, but you're *saying it to yourself*, to the part of you imagining what it would be like to be this other person.

And if you're frightened because you're reading about the latest catastrophes in the newspaper again, then you can do the same thing. Ask yourself, 'If I had caused that, why would I have done it?' Heal this part of yourself. In this way you're at least contributing to what you want to experience and achieve, rather than feeding the fear around what you don't want to happen.

How Do You Communicate Love?

Being able to communicate love is an important skill and we (Manfred and I) still practise hard at it. The more we communicate love, the more we strengthen it within ourselves – and in this way we strengthen one of the most powerful feelings there is in the world.

But how do you communicate love? Luckily this is very easy and doesn't require any great mental effort. We therefore end this book with the simplest of exercises. Because often the simplest things have the most power. Take, for example, healing plants: the most powerful ones are the most common, and so the queen of healing plants is the stinging nettle. Lots of things that may seem too pedestrian and simple are often the best that life has to offer.

To get back to love and how to communicate it: imagine a professional musician. He is technically the best in the world and he is giving a concert. Unfortunately, although he is technically the best musician in the world, the applause from the audience is muted and he doesn't understand why; he's the best, after all, so why aren't they cheering?

Now little Joe comes on stage as entertainment in the interval. He plays the same instrument as our professional, but he can only play three chords. But he plays these three chords with deep inner joy and enthusiasm. The audience goes wild and gives him a standing ovation.

'Hey, what's going on, what's got into them all of a sudden?' our super professional asks himself. 'Simple,' as Duncan Lorien, one of the most amazing music experts in the world and whose example this is, would answer. 'The professional is just reeling the music off, but the child has communicated with the music – and that is the whole point of music.' (Anyone who wants to learn how to express their feelings though music and/or to compose their own music, regardless of whether they are a complete musical novice or a professional, can learn how to do it with Duncan Lorien in two weekends. His seminars are absolutely amazing. See www.dlorien.com and www.musik-verstehen.de.)

We can apply this in a very similar way to communicating feeling in daily life. It isn't about whether we do this in a technically perfect way, but rather how much emotion we give to it. Our feeling transmits itself automatically and transmits new 'overtones' whatever we say and do.

Overtones? Yes. To compare it to music again, the colour and quality of the sound of a piano, for example, are heard in the overtones it creates (higher notes that resonate in harmony with each tone that is played). A cheap piano creates overtones that are sterile or that sound cheap somehow. An expensive piano does nothing more than create different overtones, or colour-tones. The effect is not sterile, boring or cheap, rather it is relaxing, strengthening, energizing. Given, of course, that the person playing the high-quality instruments matches it and has the ability to really communicate with music. In an equally magical way, these colour-tones also change depending on what attitude the player has internally. Bashing off the notes or enthusiastically vibrating internally with them makes an audible difference even to the novice listener.

Back to living out love in your daily life. You give everything that you do a different 'colour-tone' or a different energy when you do it with love. This alone is a form of communication.

- Food will take on different 'taste-colours' and will even smell differently, depending on what internal attitude it was cooked with.
- Your non-verbal communication (tone, body-language, expression) will contain a different 'colour-tone', depending on your internal attitude.
- The energy 'between the lines' of your letters and emails, even texts, will be richer the more authentic you are.
- Maybe you can't sing, or you keep hitting the wrong note? Never mind! Every note that is sung with love, however off-key, contains a healing sequence of overtones that work.

- Green fingers: a phenomenon of non-verbal communication with plants. They feel your love.
- Do children or animals love you? Why? Because they feel your heart.
- You can act in a play and make everyone start yawning, or you can get an amazing response with exactly the same text if you play your part with love and joy.
- Your house is always tidy, fine, but others will only feel comfortable in it if things are arranged with love. Your higher self automatically expresses your vibrations in the harmony of each room, completely independent of any conscious control on your part.

Summary

Everything you do, say, sing, move, build and plan contains your vibrations. They express themselves in a kind of harmonious colour-tone in everything you do. In order to communicate love, you simply have to be love. Love then communicates itself automatically.

Listening is the spirit of cosmic-oneness, which is attracted by vibrations just as the rest of the natural world is. With these vibrations the cosmos has only one thing in mind – to send you support for the fulfilment of your wishes as quickly as possible!

We wish you:

- a positive basic feeling in life
- love and a wonderful connection to the elemental power in everything you do

- the ability to live fully experiencing feelings in the moment, without identifying yourself with them totally
- an open heart and an appreciation of the cosmic oneness in everything
- your own individual, happy and fulfilled life.

Appendix

A Reading-Feeling Meditation

This text comes from the healing medium Ramona Rosenstein (www.rastoa.de). She wrote this for me (Barbel) at a time when I wasn't generating very many positive feelings.

I enjoyed it so much that I had the idea straightaway of making a new reading-feeling meditation from it. This is how it works:

Sit quietly with this text and just read a couple of sentences. Then close your eyes and let the words take their effect on you; sense inside yourself what feelings they release. In this way you can go at your own pace.

The Voyage of the Butterfly

Sit upright and breathe deeply and regularly. Breathe deeply in and out and concentrate on your breathing. Let go! Every time you breathe out, let everything go. Nothing and nobody can take this wonderful moment away from you.

Close your eyes for a moment and feel what's within you while you breathe.

While you're reading these lines, a transfer of energy will start to take place for your absolute wellbeing. Remember to breathe deeply in and out all the while.

Just imagine that it's possible. Just imagine that energy is transferring itself to you from well-meaning energy sources, beings and the elemental power. Just by imagining this, you increase your sense of wellbeing. From now on I'll leave you alone to decide when and where you want to pause to let the words you read work on you and make themselves felt within you!

A butterfly flutters just in front of your nose and asks you: 'Can you smell the meadow flowers? Breathe in and take all of the healing power of these flowers and plants into yourself. Breathe deeply, in complete love.

'Can you see all the colours that are all around us? Just look, go on, look! Absorb all the colours. Now!'

At this point you notice that the butterfly is shedding tears for you, because it loves you sooo much. Can you see them?

You stroke it and say: 'Hey, I love you too, and am very happy that I'm allowed to be here with you

now. I feel your love and power flowing through you and into me. Here and now, in this precise moment. Thank you.'

The butterfly flutters off with deep joy into the sea of flowers.

Are you still thinking about it? If you close your eyes, can you still feel the images and feelings?

You turn in a circle, raise your arms towards the heavens, and even the clouds smile down upon you and your delightful heart.

You call out, smiling: 'I am free, free, free.' And with each breath you feel the freedom within you, filling you with healing and peace. Take it as if there were nothing else in the world. Right now, this instant.

The butterfly now settles on your nose and looks at you with love in its eyes and says: 'You are so beautiful and sooo kind, where are you from? I have never seen you here before in this paradise. If you weren't here now, we would miss you in our world of inner peace.'

You answer: 'Do you know, I had forgotten that my home is here?' Stop and think about this.

The butterfly strokes its wings over your nose and continues to speak: 'You're very important to us

*here. You're also important to yourself. Let all of
your stress go and give free rein to your feeling.
Yes, let it flow away, so that you can feel free again.
Sometimes people forget themselves when they are
searching, because they would like to forget their
body. It's a divine present, a divine vessel. Carry
it and protect it as if it were your most precious
treasure. Rest here whenever you need to. We will
look forward to seeing you and will happily give
you wonderful energy and time, dear being. You are
always most welcome.'*

*Breathe deeply and thank the butterfly for its time
and gifts, for its love and healing.*

*Oh, what's that? A huge bubble is floating just
above your head. Oh, now it's raining down gold
dust and a myriad of coloured stars on you. You
shout for joy and catch as many as you can. The
stars jump and dance with you. Oh, how beautiful
it all is.*

*Stay with this image a moment. Then bring your
attention slowly back to here and now.*

Thanks to Ramona for her permission to use this text, and
the best of luck to all who use this 'reading-feeling-medi-
tation'. – Barbel Mohr

Contact Barbel: www.baerbelmohr.de
Contact Manfred: gefuehle@gmx.net

Titles of Related Interest

You Can Heal Your Life, the movie,
starring Louise L. Hay & Friends
(available as a 1-DVD set and
an expanded 2-DVD set)
Watch the trailer at www.LouiseHayMovie.com

*****

Cosmic Ordering for Beginners,
by Barbel Mohr and Clemens Maria Mohr

The Cosmic Ordering Wish Book 2008,
by Barbel Mohr

Cosmic Ordering Oracle Cards,
by Barbel Mohr

We hope you enjoyed this Hay House book.
If you would like to receive a free catalogue featuring additional
Hay House books and products, or if you would like information
about the Hay Foundation, please contact:

Hay House UK Ltd
292B Kensal Rd • London W10 5BE
Tel: (44) 20 8962 1230; Fax: (44) 20 8962 1239
www.hayhouse.co.uk

***

Published and distributed in the United States of America by:
Hay House, Inc. • PO Box 5100 • Carlsbad, CA 92018-5100
Tel.: (1) 760 431 7695 or (1) 800 654 5126;
Fax: (1) 760 431 6948 or (1) 800 650 5115
www.hayhouse.com

Published and distributed in Australia by:
Hay House Australia Ltd • 18/36 Ralph St • Alexandria NSW 2015
Tel.: (61) 2 9669 4299; Fax: (61) 2 9669 4144
www.hayhouse.com.au

Published and distributed in the Republic of South Africa by:
Hay House SA (Pty) Ltd • PO Box 990 • Witkoppen 2068
Tel./Fax: (27) 11 467 8904 • www.hayhouse.co.za

Published and distributed in India by:
Hay House Publishers India • Muskaan Complex • Plot No.3
B-2 • Vasant Kunj • New Delhi – 110 070.
Tel.: (91) 11 41761620; Fax: (91) 11 41761630.
www.hayhouse.co.in

Distributed in Canada by:
Raincoast • 9050 Shaughnessy St • Vancouver, BC V6P 6E5
Tel.: (1) 604 323 7100; Fax: (1) 604 323 2600

***

Sign up via the Hay House UK website to receive the Hay House
online newsletter and stay informed about what's going on with
your favourite authors. You'll receive bimonthly announcements
about discounts and offers, special events, product highlights,
free excerpts, giveaways, and more!
www.hayhouse.co.uk